London Bus Routes
ONE BY ONE
201–300

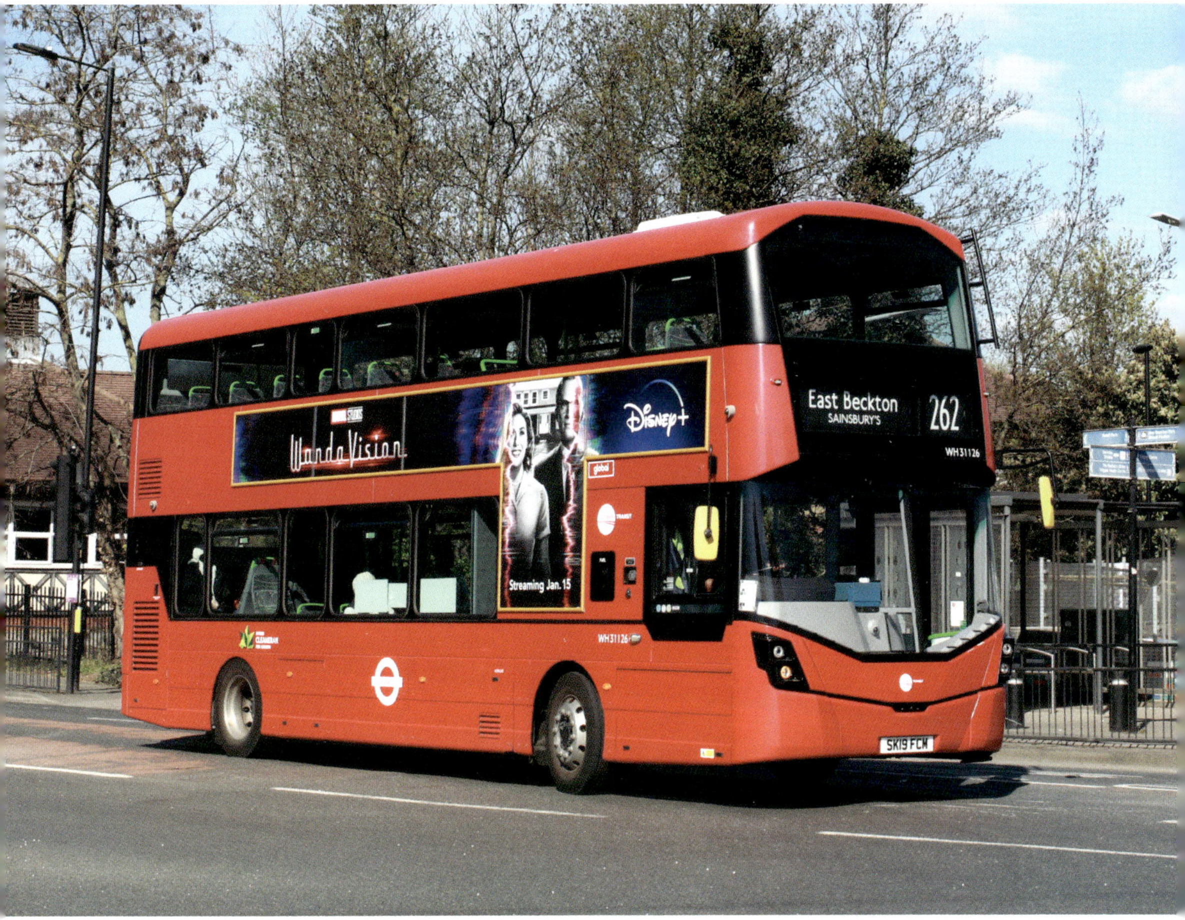

MATTHEW WHARMBY

KEY Books

TRANSPORT SYSTEMS SERIES, VOLUME 5

Front cover: In recent decades, London bus routes have shrunk and shrunk, due to the capital's relentless traffic. South-west London suburban route 200 was split in 2005, its northern section becoming 201, and today it is operated by Abellio with Alexander Dennis E20Ds like Beddington Cross-based **8821** (YY64 TZR), seen approaching the 201's modern-day Morden terminus on 16 July 2021.

Back cover: Traditionally, route numbers above 299 were reserved for London Transport's Country Area green buses, but with the hiving off of that arm to London Country in 1970, and the need for more and shorter routes in the 1980s, the series was mined heavily. The 300 was new in 1993 as a minibus route in the East Ham area, and today is Docklands Transit's responsibility out of Silvertown garage. **SE 97** (SN11 FGD) is an Alexander Dennis E20D and on 25 March 2021 is captured approaching Beckton bus station, relocated in recent years to a new and larger site directly opposite the DLR terminus.

Title page: In the early years of low-floor double-deckers, DAF was a solid third contender to Dennis and Volvo's market dominance, but the integral Wrightbus Streetdeck of two generations later has had only niche success. In 2019 Tower Transit unusually bought some for routes 262 and 473, and on 17 April 2021 Lea Interchange garage's **WH 31126** (SK19 FCM) is seen at Beckton.

Opposite: Busy south-east London suburban route 208 was one of two routes carved out of an even stronger predecessor, the old 94, in 1982. It has only recently passed to Metrobus after spending its first three and a half decades with Catford and/or Bromley garages, latterly of Stagecoach Selkent. Go-Ahead owns Metrobus and numbers its vehicles in common with the group's other companies; **EH 316** (YW19 VPJ), built in Scarborough and thus registered there, is an Alexander Dennis E40H, seen in Bromley on 17 April 2021.

Key Books
an imprint of Key Publishing Ltd.
PO Box 100
Stamford
Lincs PE19 1XQ

Copyright © Matthew Wharmby, 2021

ISBN 978 1 80282 132 1

All rights reserved. Reproduction in whole or in part in any form whatsoever or by any means is strictly prohibited without the prior permission of the Publisher.

www.keypublishing.com

Typeset by Matthew Wharmby

Introduction

Here is a snapshot of Transport for London (TfL) bus routes 201 to 300, taken during their most recent contracts. As explained in the two previous volumes in this series, but reiterated for completeness, TfL offers out each route to competitive tender for a period of five years, specifying a red livery, plus the route details and timetable, but largely leaving it up to the bidders as to what type of bus is specified and its chosen interior. When tendering was introduced in 1985, bids were awarded mostly on cost grounds, but a quality imperative has since taken precedence, together with a more recent drive to phase out fossil fuel-powered vehicles.

As the end of a route's contract approaches, TfL looks at its performance figures and decides whether to add two more years to the existing term or re-tender it; this doesn't necessarily have any bearing on whether the incumbent (if they bid) is awarded a successive contract or a newcomer is chosen. Some routes can thus stay with one company for years, and others bounce back and forth. Tendering has promoted a 'canned' sort of competition and is thus reasonably stable, even if employees risk their livelihoods being cut out from underneath them every five to seven years (a worry that has been addressed in recent years by TUPE legislation).

From 2022 TfL will be awarding all routes on the basis of fixed seven-year contracts, which will make investment in electric and/or hydrogen buses more cost-effective. Already several routes have been converted, with Alexander Dennis providing China's BYD with a foothold into the country and a strong position thereafter. Optare are also serious contenders, whilst Wrightbus, managing to stay British-owned after near-collapse in 2019, are leaders in hydrogen technology.

Matthew Wharmby
Walton-on-Thames
September 2021

201

Morden Station, Morden Road, Mitcham, Mitcham Lane, Streatham, Streatham Hill, Upper Tulse Hill, Tulse Hill Station, West Dulwich, Herne Hill Station.

ABELLIO (BC) – Alexander Dennis E20D

It was decided in 1995 to split the 200 in half, the eastern half being relaunched as 201 and sharing Merton-based Dennis Darts (DPLs) with the former parent route. In 2000 both were won on tender by Mitcham Belle and given new Dart SLFs in white, red and blue. Two extensions lengthened the 201 in 2001; one from Mitcham to Morden and, at the other end, from Tulse Hill to Herne Hill. Mitcham Belle struggled with reliability issues, but the successor operator Centra, founded in 2004, managed to be even worse, and in 2006 the 201 was reassigned to East Thames Buses, TfL's fire-brigade operator created to rescue the routes of failing contractors. It used DWL-class DAF SB120s based at Mandela Way. East Thames Buses was sold to Go-Ahead in 2009 and the buses gained London General grey skirts before moving with the 201 to Merton garage. In 2014 Abellio won the 201 on tender and introduced new E20Ds out of Beddington Cross garage.

LEFT: The driver of 8829 (YY64 YJL) has already set the bus's blinds for the return journey as it draws up to the 201's Morden terminus on 24 April 2021.

BELOW: Some alteration to the road layout at Mitcham in recent years has improved throughput of buses and the general atmosphere for pedestrians; on 7 July 2019 Beddington Cross's 8830 (YY64 YJM) is passing through.

202

Crystal Palace, Wells Park Road, Sydenham, Bell Green, Catford, Brownhill Road, Lee Green, Blackheath Village, Blackheath (Royal Standard).

ARRIVA LONDON SOUTH (N) – Alexander Dennis E40H (HT)

Designed to combine the top end of the 75 with the bottom end of the 108B when it was introduced in 1991, the 202's major selling point was its introduction of a bus service to Wells Park Road in Sydenham, and thus needed minibuses (MAs and MRLs from Plumstead, with Catford MWs on Sundays until 1994). In 1996, with Stagecoach Selkent now the inheritor of London Buses Ltd in this area, new DAL-class Darts came into service, and in 2001 these gave way to Dart SLFs. Catford garage took over operations in 2003 and continued until the tender was lost to Metrobus in 2008; the new contractor used MAN 12.240s based at Croydon. After a spate of double-deck appearances, it was decided upon the retained Metrobus contract of 2015 to order new Volvo B5LHs (WHVs). However, in 2020 Arriva London South won the 202 and this company's complement, operated out of Norwood garage, comprises Alexander Dennis E40Hs (HTs).

RIGHT: Sydenham station on 6 February 2021 sees Norwood's HT 17 (SK70 BVA) passing through.

BELOW: HT 3 (SK20 BGE) is at Blackheath Village on 6 February 2021. The rest of this batch of what will probably be Arriva London's last diesel-based double-deckers were delivered to Croydon for the 405.

203

Hounslow (Bus Station), Hounslow West, Great South West Road, Hatton Cross, Bedfont, Stanwell, Ashford Hospital, Staines (Bus Station).

LONDON UNITED (AV) – Mercedes-Benz Citaro (MCL)

New in 1951, the 203 started as a Hounslow-Hanworth link with STLs from Hounslow garage; there were soon extensions west to Hatton Cross and south-east to Twickenham. In 1952 it was pushed on westward to Bedfont, gradually forming the basis of the modern route; 1955 saw it extended further to Staines. RTs took over in 1954, but already economies were coming; the vestigial Sunday service introduced in 1956 was converted to OMO RF in 1965, reallocated to Fulwell in 1966 and withdrawn in 1969. In 1970 the 203 was withdrawn between Hounslow and Twickenham, that section passing to new route 202; conversely, the Saturday service flowered with an extension to Richmond. That fell away in 1972 when OMO SMSs took over the 203, which continued to operate in tandem with the 203A until 1976; LSs took over that year. In 1978 there came an extension from Hounslow to Brentford. In 1986 London Buses Ltd created a low-cost unit called Westllink and gave it the 203 to operate from a base at Hounslow Heath, but routine tendering saw it awarded to London Buslines in 1991 and treated to minibuses; the Brentford extension now disappeared. Darts took over in 1996, but another operator change introduced Tellings-Golden Miller in 2001, using Dart SLFs. This company was taken over by Travel London and repainted its white buses red in the five years it ran the 203, but in 2006 London United won and Hounslow garage returned. Between now and 2011 it operated Dart SLFs (DPs), but for the contract retention in 2011 new Mercedes-Benz Citaros (MCLs) were introduced, and these endure.

LEFT: A new out-thrust bus stop at Hounslow permits perfect nearside shots, such as this one of MCL 30305 (BD11 LWS) on 5 April 2021.

BELOW: With new blinds and numberplates at Hatton Cross on 11 July 2021 is Hounslow's MCL 30302 (BD11 LWO).

204

Sudbury Town Station, Wembley Central, Preston Road, Kingsbury, Colindale Avenue, Grahame Park, Burnt Oak, Edgware Station.

METROLINE (EW) – Alexander Dennis Enviro400 (TE)

New in 1990, the 204 with Edgware Ms replaced the furthest-flung extent of the 226, which itself had taken over from the 79 in 1984. An advantage of the shorter format was that it was soon extended full-time from Burnt Oak to Edgware. Darts (DRs) were introduced in 1992 and North Wembley garage took over in 1993. Under Metroline (privatised in 1994) the 204 was converted to low-floor Dart SLF (DLs) in 1997, and in 2002 a renewed Metroline contract saw double-deckers restored in the form of VPLs (Volvo B7TLs), operated once again by Edgware. The next contract in 2007 was furnished by new Enviro400s (TEs) and these remained past 2012 as well. Metroline kept hold of the 204 in 2017 but the following year reallocated it to Alperton (one of the ex-First garages now part of Metroline West); some TEs went with it, but Alperton was a VW (Volvo B9TL) operator and these became predominant. Upon Alperton's closure later in 2021, Edgware TEs resumed control.

RIGHT: The first phase of Alperton garage's closure saw the 204 restored to Edgware garage. On 5 September 2021 TE 1095 (LK60 AHC) is emerging from the station entrance.

BELOW: On 5 September 2021 TE 1103 (LK60 AHP), transferred from Alperton back to Edgware with the 204 the previous day, is negotiating extensive roadworks as it makes the left turn onto the main drag.

205

Paddington, Marylebone, Baker Street, Euston, King's Cross, Angel, Old Street, Shoreditch, Liverpool Street, Aldgate, Whitechapel, Mile End, Bow Church.

STAGECOACH EAST LONDON (BW) – Alexander Dennis E40H

The successful northern half of the old Stationlink, the 205 began in 2002 with Metroline TPs based at Cricklewood; it soon transferred to Perivale. In 2007 it was extended from Whitechapel to Mile End, and its tender offer took it to East London in 2009; this company in its interregnum between two periods of Stagecoach ownership deployed new Scanias based at Bow. An extension to Bow Church was implemented at the same time. In 2014 Stagecoach retained the 205 on tender and converted it to hybrid E40Hs, which continue today.

LEFT: On 15 September 2020 Bow's 12320 (SK14 CSY) is crossing Mile End junction.

206

Kilburn Park Station, Queens Park, Brondesbury Park, Willesden, Harlesden, Brent Park, Wembley Trading Estate, Wembley Park (The Paddocks).

METROLINE WEST (WJ) –Alexander Dennis E20D (DEL)

Deriving from a short-lived Brondesbury-area 172 and before that, the top end of the 176, the 206 was new in 1990 with Willesden DTs. North Wembley took over in 1995 and, under Metroline, phased in DSD-class Dart SLFs in 2002 and MM-class MAN 12.240s in 2007; these moved to Perivale in 2009. In 2011 the 206 was rerouted to Wembley Park rather than St Raphaels, and in 2012 was taken over by First with new DMVs (E20Ds) from Willesden Junction garage. After First's takeover in 2013 these became known as DELs.

LEFT: Willesden Junction's DEL 1979 (YX12 ATF), seen in Harlesden on 10 December 2019, was new as First DMV 44311.

207

White City (Bus Station), Shepherd's Bush, Acton Vale, Acton, Ealing Broadway, West Ealing, Hanwell, Southall, Hayes By-Pass.

ABELLIO (GW) – Alexander Dennis Enviro400, E40D and E40H

Trolleybus route 607 gave way to Hanwell RM-operated 207 in 1960, this instant powerhouse fielding 52 buses. Uxbridge gained a Sunday share in 1961 and then expanded it to daily in 1963. The route was busy enough to take RMLs in 1967, but in 1976 both garages received DMs. The doored buses, however, proved as unsuccessful on the 207 as elsewhere and in 1980 RMLs returned, first from Hanwell and later from Uxbridge. OPO was the next cost-saver and the 207 succumbed in 1987 using Ms. In 1993 Hanwell closed, its allocation passing to Acton Tram Depot, and in 2000, six years after both had become Centrewest companies (and later First), TNL-class Tridents took over. In 2001 thoughts of artic conversion were entertained with experimental use of Volvo B7LAs and B10LAs allocated to Greenford, and in 2005 this took place throughout, although the Acton–Uxbridge section was separated as 427. The 207 was now operated with EAs (Mercedes-Benz Citaro Gs) from Hayes, but the bendies proved as unwelcome a sea change as the DMs had been, and at the end of 2011 came Scania double-deckers. In 2013 First sold its operations to Metroline, which in 2017 replaced the Scanias with Volvo B9TLs, but in 2019 Abellio won and restocked the 207 with existing E40Ds plus new E40Hs.

RIGHT: E40H 2005 (YX19 ORL), seen in Ealing on 21 April 2019, was one of five new buses bought by Abellio to support a disparate collection of existing E40Ds. At first it ran from Hayes but was later put into the new garage at Southall.

BELOW: On 20 July 2020 9527 (SN12 AAZ) is heading west through Ealing, having been new to the C2 but made spare after that route's withdrawal.

208

Lewisham (Town Centre), Catford, Bellingham, Downham, Bromley, Southborough, Petts Wood, Crofton Lane, Orpington (Perry Hall Road).

METROBUS (MB) – Alexander Dennis E40H (EH)

Taking the Catford-allocated portion of the 94 when introduced in 1982, the 208 became the busiest new route locally. Even so, crew operation was dwindling and in 1984 the RMs were replaced by crew Ts, which lost their conductors a year later. In 1986 Bromley took over, relegating Catford to Saturdays, but a year later Bromley became Sunday to Friday and Catford returned briefly on weekdays; this was also when the Saturday extension to Surrey Docks was taken off. In 1990 Catford withdrew altogether, but returned in 1993 to oust Bromley. With the route operating in two overlapping sections (Lewisham-Bromley Common and Catford-Orpington), the southern section was given LV-class Dennis Lances in 1994, shortly before privatisation of the operating LBL subsidiary as Stagecoach Selkent. The LVs left for the 227 in 1997 and Bromley was added again. In 2000 Catford exited once more and Bromley received new Tridents. The sectional format came to an end in 2010 and Stagecoach Selkent's contract of 2012 specified new E40Ds. However, a new operator beckoned in 2019 when Metrobus won the 208; new E40Hs (EH class) were put into service from Orpington garage.

LEFT: On 28 February 2021 Orpington's EH 326 (YW19 VPV) is seen in Bromley High Street.

BELOW: EH 311 (YW19 VPC) makes the right turn from Kentish Way into Elmfield Road, Bromley, on 17 April 2021.

209

Mortlake (Avondale Road), Barnes Bridge Station, Barnes Pond, Barnes Common, Hammersmith Bridge (South Side).

LONDON GENERAL (AF) – Alexander Dennis E20D (SE)

A renumbering of Dart-operated Mortlake shuttle 9A in 1997, the 209, with its Shepherd's Bush-operated DRs of London United, omitted its precedessor's section beyond Hammersmith to Kensington. From 1998 it also had a Fulwell allocation and a quantity of DTs. Armchair took over in 1999 and the bifurcation introduced in 1994 to Harrodian School became the 609. Armchair's fare was orange and white Dart SLFs based at Brentford, and barring an operator acquisition (by Metroline) it stayed put for two more decades. These buses became the DA class and were replaced in 2011 by transferred DPs. DEs (Enviro200s) are the modern complement, but the 209 suffered from ongoing problems with Hammersmith Bridge, as did all routes crossing it. The latest, semi-permanent closure from 2019 obliged the route to turn at the top end of Castelnau instead, after a brief attempt to divert it to Putney Bridge Station that ultimately resulted in the creation of new route 378. Both this and the 209 are now operated by London General with SEs from Putney.

RIGHT: On 24 July 2021 Putney's SE 293 (YW19 VSG) is passing through Barnes Village, as the 209's predecessor 9A had done before it, and prior to that the long-lived 9.

BELOW: Having looped around the top of Castelnau short of Hammersmith Bridge, SE 296 (YW19 VSL) is on its way south on a blistering hot 18 July 2021.

210

Finsbury Park Station, Stroud Green, Hornsey Rise, Archway, Highgate Village, Hampstead Heath, Golders Green, Brent Cross Shopping Centre.

METROLINE (W) – Alexander Dennis Enviro400 (TE) and E40H (TEH)

Linking Golders Green and Finsbury Park over the top of Hampstead Heath and Highgate since time immemorial, the 210 has had to be single-deck until only recently. Muswell Hill was the traditional operating garage, with help along the way from the original Holloway, Tottenham and Leyton, the last coming on in 1963 when the 210 was extended on Sunday over the 236 to Leyton. RFs were in charge between 1952 and 1971, with their condctors removed in 1968. Holloway was added in 1970 and joined Muswell Hill in receiving SMSs in 1971; the Sunday extension was pulled back to Finsbury Park at the same time. In 1976 the 210 was projected at the other end to the new Brent Cross Shopping Centre. LSs replaced the SMSs in 1978 and Holloway withdrew in 1986, only to supplant Muswell Hill altogether in 1986, with National 2s (the most modern version of the LS). In 1990 Grey-Green took over under tender, with Volvo B10Ms, lasting until Thorpes was awarded control in 1998, using yellow and red Dart SLFs. Thorpes was then acquired by Metroline in 2004. The most significant change of the modern era was the 210's double-decking in 2008 with Tridents (TAs); in 2009 it was reallocated from Perivale to Cricklewood and a year later given TEs (Enviro400s). TEHs and VWHs have also appeared lately.

LEFT: A wintry but sunny 25 February 2018 at Finsbury Park sees Cricklewood's E40H hybrid TEH 1453 (LK13 BGV) about to turn at the end of another route 210 journey.

BELOW: An earlier hybrid new to Cricklewood, TEH 1107 (LK60 AHV) is seen at Archway on 3 November 2020.

211

Waterloo Station, Westminster Bridge, Victoria, Sloane Square, Fulham Broadway, Dawes Road, Hammersmith (Bus Station).

LONDON UNITED (V) – Wrightbus New Routemaster (LT)

This fifth incarnation of the number 211 was introduced in 1993 as a way to partially one-man the 11 by clipping its western end off past Fulham Broadway. It then provided a better link to Waterloo than the previous Red Arrow 511 had done. DRL-class Darts were in charge from Victoria Basement until Stockwell took over late in the 211's first year. Tendering took it to Travel London in 1998, with new Optare Excels, after which Limebourne acquired this part of the operation in 2000, only for Connex Bus to scoop it all up the following year. Under Connex, double-deckers were added in the form of new Dennis Tridents. In 2004 a rerouting via Chelsea and Westminster Hospital was implemented, diverging from the 11 here. That year also saw Connex pass to National Express, which resuscitated the Travel London brand, but in 2009 a new identity was introduced; Abellio. Contract renewal in 2012 was accomplished with new E40Ds, and in 2017 the route was selected for conversion to Borismaster operation. As this was done mid-contract, the buses themselves had to move to London United when that company won the 211 in 2019. Stamford Brook garage is in charge.

RIGHT: Mid-route at Victoria on 1 July 2020 is Stamford Brook's LT 670 (LTZ 1670). This Borismaster is actually onto its third operator, having begun on London Central's 68 but then passing with that route to Abellio before pitching up at London United for the 211.

BELOW: One of London United's original Borismasters, LT 82 (LTZ 1082) is at Hammersmith on 10 December 2019.

212

St. James Street Station, Walthamstow Central, Fulbourne Road, Highams Park, Chingford Hatch, Friday Hill, Chingford Station.

LONDON GENERAL (NP) – BYD DD (Ee)

New in 1981 to replace the eastern side of the circular W21, the 212 bowed with Walthamstow DMSs and had received Ts by the end of that year. In 1982 it was projected from Walthamstow Central to Yardley Lane Estate, becoming an unwieldy U-shape. From 1987 to 1988 its Sunday service was reallocated to Leyton and shared LSs with the 236, which was extended up to the area in accompaniment. The 212 resumed its original format in 1988, the western leg now becoming the 215. In 1991 it was taken over by Capital Citybus at Northumberland Park with new yellow Leyland Olympians, which became red when Capital Citybus was taken over by First in 1998. 2000 saw Dart SLFs (DMLs) take over; first red and white ones meant for Tramlink support, then its own batch. In 2005 it was reallocated to Hackney but returned to Northumberland Park in 2009, just after double-deckers returned in the form of TNs. A contract award in 2010 placed the 212 with CT Plus using Scanias, but the newcomers lasted only one term and Tower Transit won in 2015, introducing new Volvo B5LHs. Just the one term was this firm's lot as well; London General won in 2020, this company having acquired Northumberland Park from First in 2013. The new vehicle complement consists of electric BYDs (Ees).

LEFT: Northumberland Park's Ee 42 (LF20 XNM) is leaving Chingford bus station on 8 October 2020.

BELOW: Swinging off Hoe Street into Selborne Road towards Walthamstow Central and beyond, using a proper junction rather than round a fiddly roundabout, is Ee 3 (LF20 XLC) on 25 June 2020.

213

Kingston (Fairfield Bus Station), Norbiton, Clarence Avenue, New Malden, Worcester Park, North Cheam, Cheam, Sutton, Sutton Garage.

LONDON GENERAL (A) – Alexander Dennis Enviro400 (DOE)

The current 213 was reconstituted in 1984 as a renumbering of the 213A; its predecessor had been best associated with the routeing via Traps Lane rather than Clarence Avenue, and thus withered until withdrawal in 1978. The new route was shared between Norbiton Ms and Sutton DMSs and had an amazing four eastern termini; Sutton Garage, St Helier, Belmont Station and West Croydon, the last on Sundays as an extension over the 154. In 1987 Sutton withdrew so that the 213 could bcome part of Norbiton's Kingston Bus network, using revived DMSs, and the extensions gradually came off; St Helier in 1988, Belmont and West Croydon in 1990. Under tender, Sutton came back but now with Ms, and has continued ever since, latterly as part of London General. Just the vehicles have changed; to NVs in 1997, EVLs in 2002 and DOEs in 2009; in the last decade, these latter have been supported by WVLs (Volvo B9TLs), Es (E40Ds) and WHVs (Volvo B5LHs) wandering from other Sutton routes.

RIGHT: On 21 March 2021 Sutton's DOE 6 (LX58 CWU) is passing Cromwell Street bus station.

BELOW: Like all fifty-four members of this class, DOE 2 (LX58 CWO), seen in Eden Street, Kingston on 11 April 2021, has been repainted all-red on refurbishment for a second set of contracts on Sutton routes 93, 154 and 213.

214

Moorgate (Finsbury Square), Old Street Station, City Road, Islington, King's Cross, Camden Town, Kentish Town, Parliament Hill Fields, Highgate Village (North Road).

LONDON GENERAL (NP) – BYD D9UR (SEe)

Replacing trolleybus route 615 in 1961, the 214 debuted with Highgate RMs, linking Parliament Hill Fields and Moorgate as it does today (with amendments). Highgate was renamed Holloway in 1971 and converted the 214 to DM in 1975; OMO DMSs came in 1981 and Metrobuses replaced the Fleetlines in 1984. In 1986 the route was reallocated to Chalk Farm, which then proceeded to replace its Ms with Ts. A shortage of Titans and surfeit of LSs by the end of the decade compelled conversion to LS in 1989, but enough Ts were gathered to restore the upper deck and furnish an extension from Moorgate to London Bridge Station. This lasted until 1992, when the 214 was rerouted to Liverpool Street and taken over on tender by Thamesway, with yellow Darts. In 1993 an extension was mounted from Parliament Hill Fields up the steep Highgate West Hill to Highgate Village, but Thamesway struggled later on, having to sub-contract weekend workings to Capital Citybus in 1998 and then surrendering the route to MTL London, which took the Darts (as DPs) until obtaining their own. These were DRLs and then DNLs, which had blue skirts added following Metroline's takeover of MTL. DL-class Dart SLFs then filtered onto the route before a new batch of DLDs arrived in 2005. These lasted until 2017, working since 2010 out of King's Cross garage. DEs then took over, but in 2019 London General was awarded the 214, putting into Northumberland Park garage with new electric BYDs (SEe class).

LEFT: Northumberland Park had worked on the 214 before, when part of Capital Citybus, but from 2019 took over permanently as a London General garage. Here at Old Street on 12 September 2019 is SEe 92 (LA19 KAU).

BELOW: SEe 80 (LA19 KBY) is mid-route at King's Cross on 17 September 2019.

215

Walthamstow Central Station, Crooked Billet, Chingford Mount, Old Church Road, Mansfield Hill, Yardley Lane Estate, Lee Valley Campsite.

STAGECOACH EAST LONDON (T) – Alexander Dennis E40D

The 215 was new in 1989 to replace the western shank of U-shaped route 212, but there had been a standalone Walthamstow Central–Yardley Lane Estate route before, known as 276. Titans from Walthamstow garage were in charge until 1991, when the London Forest strike obliged Walthamstow to close and Capital Citybus took over with Metrobuses based at Northumberland Park. The route had by now commenced summer season runs to and from the Lee Valley Camp Site right at the northern edge of the map. Capital Citybus lasted nineteen years on the 215, becoming known as First Capital in 1998 and putting out Olympians, then Tridents. Stagecoach East London won in 2010 and bought five new Scanias to work out out of Leyton, but it was liable to field just as many Tridents; later, E40Ds eventually replaced the Tridents and Scanias and continue to work today.

RIGHT: The approaches to Walthamstow Central bus station have been tidied up, certainly (if unintentionally) to the benefit of bus photographers wanting unobstructed nearsides. Here on 24 November 2019 is Leyton's 10114 (LX12 DDA), representing the 215's current output since the end of Tridents three months earlier.

BELOW: 19870 (LX12 DAA) is making the simplified right turn towards the bus station on 11 March 2020.

216

Kingston (Cromwell Road Bus Station), Hampton Court, Sunbury Village, Sunbury Cross, Ashford, Ashford Hospital (Stanwell Road), Staines (Bus Station).

LONDON UNITED (HH) – Alexander Dennis E20D (DLE)

Linking Kingston and Staines via Sunbury for over eighty years, the 216 was peripheral enough to fall out of the system altogether at one point, through it has since returned to TfL status and is tendered like the rest. For its first forty years it was operated by Kingston garage, using LTLs until 1949, TDs until 1959 and RFs thereafter, with OMO introduced in 1964. 1976 saw the RFs replaced by BLs and in 1982 Norbiton garage took over with LSs, at which point the Staines terminus was changed from Bridge Street to the new bus station. An unusual extension pushed the 216 south from Kingston over the 211 to Tolworth between 1983 and 1987, whilst for many years there was a summer Sunday extension from Staines to Thorpe Park. Later in 1987 the 216 was transferred to the Westlink unit, which had reopened Kingston garage, but in 1995 that company (privatised in 1994) reallocated it briefly to Hounslow Heath. Under management ownership, then that of West Midlands Travel and finally London United, Westlink completed eighteen years with LSs and then converted the 216 to DWLs in 2000; Kingston closed finally and Hounslow Heath took over. A short-term contract was held with Tellings-Golden Miller between 2002 and 2003, using Optare Excels, but London United returned and purchased DPS-class Dart SLFs. In recent years it has bounced round the garages, serving at Fulwell (2006–15), Hounslow Heath (2015–16) and back to Fulwell, which since 2018 has used new E20Ds (DLE class). In 2021 it struck up a new allocation at Hounslow Heath, taking its DLEs with it.

LEFT: On 9 May 2021 DLE 30225 (YX18 KVO), newly transferred from Fulwell to Hounslow Heath with the 216, is seen leaving Kingston.

BELOW: Coming up to Kingston on 9 May 2021 is DLE 30217 (YX18 KVE), not yet wearing its new Hounslow Heath garage code.

217

Turnpike Lane Station, Westbury Avenue, Edmonton (Cambridge), Great Cambridge Road, Carterhatch (Halfway House), Waltham Cross (Bus Station).

SULLIVAN BUSES (SM) – Alexander Dennis E40D (E)

A fixture up and down the Great Cambridge Road from Turnpike Lane since 1954, the 217 has mostly been in the hands of Enfield garage and for many years ran on beyond the border at Waltham Cross to serve Upshire. OMO DMSs replaced its RTs in 1977 and Ms followed in 1981. It abandoned Upshire in 1982 but between 1989 and 1990 served Hammond Street instead. Potters Bar took over in 1990, introducing DMLs in 1998, TPs in 2003 and TEs in 2014, before what had become Metroline's streak was broken in 2017 by Sullivan Buses. New E40Ds (Es) entered service at this time.

RIGHT: E 71 (AW17 SUL), seen at Turnpike Lane on 24 April 2021, is one of the batch of Sullivan Buses E40Ds with personalised registrations; the company also specifies the red-based TfL moquette and gold handrails, not unlike those used on the Borismaster.

218

Hammersmith (Bus Station), Askew Road, Acton Vale, Acton, Twyford Avenue, Noel Road, Gypsy Corner, North Acton Station.

TOWER TRANSIT (X) – Alexander Dennis E20D (DML)

New in 2019, this route assisted the 306 in covering the 266's withdrawn Acton–Hammersmith leg and then took over the 440's backstreets as far as North Acton. A batch of second-time-leased E20Ds (DMLs) is in charge, operating from Westbourne Park garage of Tower Transit.

RIGHT: On 12 December 2020 Westbourne Park's DML 44183 (YX11 AEY) finds itself at Acton. This bus was new to First as DML 44182, passing to Metroline West as DE 1900 but then being leased back by Tower Transit, who forgot its orginal fleetnumber and applied a new one that's out by one unit!

219

Wimbledon Station, South Wimbledon, Merton, Colliers Wood, Tooting Broadway, Tooting Bec, Wandsworth Common, Trinity Road, Clapham Junction (Asda).

LONDON GENERAL (AL) – Wrightbus Streetlite (WS)

Commissioned in 1987 with the aim of saving a little money on conductors' wages, the 219 combined the Clapham Junction–Tooting Bec end of the 19 with the Tooting–Mitcham end of the 88, operating DMSs from Merton. As time went on each end was changed, with the northern terminus becoming South Kensington in 1989 and the southern one being amended to Colliers Wood in 1991, by which time Metrobuses were in charge. In 1993 the 219 was pulled back across the river to Battersea and in 1995 to the more logical Clapham Junction, the other end also being amended again with a withdrawal between Tooting Broadway and Colliers Wood. In 1996 it received Darts (DWs) and two years later it was extended to St George's Hospital in Tooting, though in 1999 it passed this section to the 155 so as to take over that busy route's leg on to Wimbledon. LDP-class Dart SLFs were ordered at this point and remained in charge, though the actual vehicles were changed once over that decade. SOEs were also in evidence between 2009 and 2013, but that year's contract retention saw WS-class Wrightbus Streetlites introduced, and these have stayed put, being put through refurbishment for another London General contract applying from 2018.

LEFT: The 'W' device on the front of Wrightbus Streetlites may not be a real radiator grille, but its removal upon refurbishment is unsettling, as though the buses have had their faces removed! Merton's WS 17 (LJ13 GKD) is leaving Clapham Junction on 12 June 2021.

BELOW: Another 'no-face' route 219 Streetlite is WS 20 (LJ13 GKG), passing through Tooting on 30 July 2020.

220

Harlesden (Willesden Junction), White City, Shepherd's Bush, Hammersmith, Fulham Palace Road, Putney Bridge Road, Wandsworth (Southside Shopping Centre).

LONDON UNITED (RP) – Alexander Dennis E40D (ADE)

Trolleybus route 630 between Park Royal Stadium and West Croydon gave way in its entirety to new route 220 in 1960, operated by Shepherd's Bush RMs. Gradually it began to fall back to the north, being cut south of Mitcham in 1966, though the northern terminus was standardised on Willesden Junction, with peak-hour journeys to Park Royal Stadium lingering until 1982. When it hosted the inaugural DMSs in 1971, the 220 was withdrawn between Tooting Station and Mitcham. Shepherd's Bush rotated its early DMSs out for B20s in 1977 and converted to M in 1983, as did the Wandsworth Sunday share added in 1981 and lasting until 1987. In 1991 the 220 was withdrawn between Wandsworth and Tooting and has held this form ever since, with just the vehicles changing, given that the operator has also remained the same (London Buses Ltd having given way to London United in 1994). A short-lived garage at Wood Lane operated DRs on the Sunday service between 1993 and 1995. Otherwise, VA-class Volvo B7TLs replaced the Metrobuses in 2000 and were themselves eased out by newer examples before a contract applying from 2012 introduced new ADE-class E40Ds. The 220 was reallocated to Park Royal garage at this point, and this base found itself physically moved to a new site in 2017.

RIGHT: ADE 40447 (YX62 BBZ) from the new Park Royal garage is coming up to the north side of Putney Bridge on 21 March 2021.

BELOW: ADH 45048 (YX62 FTP) represents the E40H type on the 220 when caught between Shepherd's Bush and Hammersmith on a sunny 18 July 2021.

221

Edgware Station, Mill Hill Broadway, Mill Hill East, Woodside Park, North Finchley, Friern Barnet, New Southgate, Bounds Green, Wood Green, Turnpike Lane Station.

ARRIVA LONDON NORTH (WN) – Wrightbus Gemini 2 (DW)

New in 1960 to replace trolleybus routes 521 and 621, the 221 originally linked Farringdon Street and North Finchley, with Finchley RMs plus on-and-off participation by Wood Green. 1966 saw an ambitious extension from North Finchley via the 125 and 240A to Edgware, making the route tremendously long, even when operated in sections. The two constituent garages were sharing work on the 221 daily by 1968, although Wood Green gained the ascendancy and continued it after DMSs replaced the RMs in 1973. Ms then took over, first at Finchley in 1980 and then at Wood Green in 1981. In 1986 Finchley came off and Edgware came on, albeit only for a year. 1992 saw the 221 cut in half, abandoning everything between Turnpike Lane and King's Cross or Holborn Circus, with some scattered early journeys surviving only until 1995. Now under Arriva London North, the 221 received DLAs in 1999, VLWs in 2009 and DWs in 2017.

LEFT: DW 478 (LJ61 CCD) was new to Wood Green for the 29 but has remained there following that route's conversion to HV; on 20 July 2020 it is seen at the Edgware end of the 221.

BELOW: The DWs transferred specifically to Wood Green for the 221 were new to Brixton garage and later refurbished; on 20 February 2021 DW 293 (LJ59 LVY) is in Wood Green.

222

Hounslow (Bus Station), Hounslow West, Cranford, Harlington Corner, Sipson Road, West Drayton, Cowley, Uxbridge Station.

METROLINE WEST (UX) – Volvo B5LH (VWH)

New in 1971, the 222 inherited the 223's old leg to Hounslow so that the latter could be diverted to Heathrow. Uxbridge operated RTs, but by the end of the year the 222 was OMO with SMSs. At the start of 1973 DMSs took over, and after their time in service had been cut short, Ms appeared in 1980. In 1989 it began to be run on a common schedule with the 223, but in 1994 it was selected for operation of the pioneering low-floor buses, LLW-class Dennis Lance SLFs. These passed to Centrewest upon privatisation that autumn and gained Uxbridge Buses fleetnames. Tendering in 2000 saw the 222 awarded to London United and taken over by DP-class Dart SLFs from Hounslow. London United won it back twice more, and for 2012 double-decked it with ADE-class E40Ds. However, in 2017 Metroline West came out victorious, restoring Uxbridge garage but this time with VWH-class Volvo B5LHs.

RIGHT: On 5 April 2021 Uxbridge's VWH 2186 (LK16 DGX) is in Hounslow, on the last leg of a typical route 222 journey to the bus station.

BELOW: Coming the other way on the same day is VWH 2175 (LK16 DFP).

| 223 | Harrow (Bus Station), Northwick Park Hospital, Kenton, South Kenton, Preston Road, Wembley Park, Wembley Stadium, Wembley Central (Montrose Crescent). |

LONDON UNITED (RP) – Alexander Dennis E20D (DLE)

Several unserved roads in South Kenton and North Wembley gained their first buses when the 223 was introduced in 1995 with MAs from Alperton (Centrewest, later known as First). DWs replaced the MAs in 1997 and DMs (Dart SLFs) took over in 2001. In 2011 new E20Ds (also called DMs) were introduced, becoming DEMs in 2013 with Metroline's takeover. Tendering in 2018 saw the 223 won by London United and new DLE-class E20Ds were introduced from Park Royal garage.

ABOVE: On one of the stands carved out of side streets adjacent to Harrow bus station is E20D DLE 30270 (YX68 UOD) on 5 January 2019. Sovereign fleetnames and Harrow garage codes are carried, but vehicles are likely to be pooled with Park Royal and the advent of common RATP Group fleetnames will mask this in future.

BELOW: Park Royal's DLE 30313 (YX68 URU) has served Harrow bus station on 18 September 2019 and is now setting off for Wembley Central.

224

St. Raphael's (Pitfield Way), Brent Park, Park Royal (Asda), Central Middlesex Hospital, Abbey Road, Heather Park, Alperton (Sainsbury's).

LONDON UNITED (RP) – Alexander Dennis E20D (DLE)

New in 1990, the 224 replaced the middle section of the 226 between Willesden Junction and North Wembley; it used Ms from Alperton before the inevitable minibussing in 1991 with MAs (Mercedes-Benz 811Ds). In 1995 it handed its roads beyond Wembley to the new 223 and later in the year was upgraded to DW-class Darts. DML-class Dart SLFs appeared in 2001. In 2006 a second double-run (there already being one via Alperton Station and Sainsbury's) was added to this route in the form of a leg to and from Iveagh Avenue in Park Royal, and in 2011, to accompany First's latest contract renewal and introduction of Enviro200s (also classified DMLs), the 224 was extended from Willesden Junction to St Raphael's to replace the 206 over this section. In 2013 First sold its operations to Metroline and the DMLs became DEs, and when the 224's tender came up again in 2018 London United won this time; the current buses are DLE-class E20Ds and the operating garage is Park Royal.

RIGHT: The Central Middlesex Hospital area is much changed, but is still an important stop for local routes to dogleg around, sometimes in a convoluted manner; northbound 224s, represented by Park Royal's DLE 30322 (YX68 UVH) on 18 July 2021, have to loop round the local ASDA and approach from the rear.

BELOW: The southbound 224 just needs to make a right turn, as DLE 30317 (YX68 UVB) is doing on 18 July 2021.

225

Hither Green Station, Hither Green Lane, Lewisham, Brookmill Road, Deptford, New Cross, Trundleys Road, Surrey Quays, Canada Water Station.

LONDON CENTRAL (MG) – Alexander Dennis E20D

New in 1989 with SRs from Catford, the 225 split in half the 181, a single-deck route that had grown too long for its own future career as a minibus route. It linked Lewisham and Rotherhithe via Surrey Quays and a circuit of the peninsula. Under tender, it was won by Kentish Bus in 1994 and provisioned with new Darts from a base at Lewisham, and managed to sidestep the trouble the new operator had got itself into by taking on too much at once. In 1994 operation was reallocated across the river to Cambridge Heath, but things got silly after Kentish Bus became an Arriva company in common ownership with Grey-Green, because in 1998 the 225 was put into distant Barking and operated out of there. Finally some sense was seen, and in 1998 it was voluntarily handed over to Stagecoach Selkent, which restored Catford garage to control with DRL-class Darts. Since 1996 the route has been diverted via Rotherhithe Street and then served Canada Water station when it opened in 1999, simultaneously adding a short extension onward to Bermondsey. In 2001 London Central won the 225, using LDP-class Dart SLFs from New Cross. For its 2006 contract it was cut back to Canada Water but pushed at the other end to Hither Green station, gaining newer LDPs. In 2018 Morden Wharf garage took it over and restocked it with mid-life E20Ds spare from Metrobus and retaining their class code-less fleetnumbers.

LEFT: In the normal scheme of things, Go-Ahead would assign an SE-class fleetnumber to a second-hand E20D, but former Metrobus 744 (YX13 AFO), seen in Lewisham on 30 June 2019, was left alone upon its transfer.

BELOW: Morden Wharf's 740 (YX13 AFF) is in Lewisham on 17 April 2021.

226

Golders Green Station, The Vale, Cricklewood, Dollis Hill, Willesden, Harlesden, Central Middlesex Hospital, Park Royal, Hanger Lane, Ealing Broadway Station.

METROLINE WEST (WJ) – Alexander Dennis Enviro200 (DE)

Very long-established on its Golders Green–Cricklewood core, the 226 was Cricklewood-operated from the outset and received STLs in 1949, followed in 1953 by the ubiquitous RTs. That year saw an extension to Park Royal; 1962 saw reallocation to Willesden with RTLs, which operated until 1968. After three years with RTs again, OMO SMSs took over in 1971. DMSs restored the upper deck in 1978 and Ms replaced them in 1980. A most unusual change in 1984 saw the 226 extended over the entirety of the withdrawn 79 to reach Burnt Oak, adding its Alperton allocation (briefly at first; it returned between 1987 and 1990). This really made it too long, despite retaining a two-section structure, and reliability faltered, so in 1990 it was withdrawn again beyond Park Royal. The through service continued on Sundays, and in 1992 DT-class Darts took over. In 1995 the whole service was standardised as Alperton–Golders Green and transferred on tender to Centrewest, which ran it with DWs from Alperton garage. Low-floors appeared in 2001 as DML-class Dart SLFs, and in 2004 the route was reallocated to Willesden Junction and extended in Park Royal to the First Central Business Park. A further extension to Ealing Broadway was carried out in 2007, followed in 2008 by new Enviro200s (also DMLs, though since 2013 they have been known as DEs following Metroline West's takeover of First's operations here).

RIGHT: On 13 December 2019 Willesden Junction's DE 1623 (YX58 FPE) is passing Willesden garage, from where the 226 used to work for many years.

BELOW: The 226 absorbed local route PR1's backstreet service to Ealing Broadway in 2007, and on 30 March 2021 DE 1632 (YX58 FPU) is coming onto stand there.

227

Crystal Palace, Crystal Palace Park Road, Penge, Clock House, Beckenham, Shortlands, Bromley North Station.

METROBUS (MB) – Wrightbus Streetlite (WS)

Extant under this number since 1934, the 227 linked Penge and Welling before losing its roads beyond Chislehurst in 1938; in 1951 it gained its best-known form with an extension from Penge to Crystal Palace and reallocation from Elmers End garage to Bromley, which always had to use single-deckers given the presence of a low bridge at Shortlands. In 1952 RFs replaced LTLs and stayed until OMO SMSs took over in 1971. LSs followed in 1977 and also enjoyed a long innings, though the very end of their tenure saw whichever were the latest minibuses at Bromley assume the Sunday service from 1991. The following year it was tendered and awarded to Kentish Bus, which won multiple awards for its reliable operation with National Greenways based at Dunton Green. Even so, the 227 formed part of a unique corporate swap in 1997 designed to restore routes closer to suitable garages, and thus returned Bromley, now under Stagecoach Selkent and using Dennis Lances (LVs). These were replaced by long-wheelbase Dart SLFs in 2000, and in 2012 a batch of Mercedes-Benz Citaros was introduced. Upon the 227's next contract offer in 2019, Metrobus emerged victorious, taking Wrightbus Streetlites to operate from Orpington.

LEFT: On 30 August 2019 Orpington's WS 119 (SK19 FBN) is manoeuvring on the outskirts of central Bromley, otherwise pedestrianised since the 1990s.

BELOW: WS 122 (SK19 FBG) is seen on 31 May 2020, coming up to the Crystal Palace terminus at the other end of the 227.

228

Maida Hill (The Chippenham), Harrow Road, Ladbroke Grove, Holland Park, Shepherd's Bush, White City, East Acton, Harlesden, Central Middlesex Hospital.

TOWER TRANSIT (X) – Wrightbus Streetlite (WV)

New in 2009, the 228 follows a convoluted path through some western parts of inner-city London, but has two previously unserved sections to itself, north of East Acton and along the southern extent of Ladbroke Grove. It began with DML-class Enviro200s operated by First's Willesden Junction garage, though in 2013 this operator was taken over by Metroline West and the buses became known as DEs. Metroline West won it again in 2014 but, after the standard five years was up, lost it to Tower Transit, which put it into Westbourne Park garage with new Wrightbus Streetlites.

RIGHT: On 11 April 2019 Westbourne Park's WV 46216 (SK17 HGX) is pulling into the Shepherd's Bush end of the Westfield White City complex. It was new to Lea Interchange for the 236 but came here after cuts to that route.

BELOW: Also coming across to the 228 (and 218) was WV 46219 (SK17 HHA), seen at Ladbroke Grove on 31 May 2021.

229

Sidcup (Queen Mary's Hospital), Sidcup, Hurst Road, Bexley, Bexleyheath, Erith, Belvedere, Abbey Road, Abbey Wood, Crossway, Thamesmead (Town Centre).

ARRIVA LONDON NORTH (DT) – Alexander Dennis E40D (T)

Growing steadily since its 1951 debut as a Sidcup-area local, the 229 quickly pushed south to Orpington and doubled its vehicle complement, operated by Sidcup garage. In 1952 came an extension at the other end, to Bexleyheath; two years later it traded its STLs for RTLs and then standardised on RTs. As part of the first stage of trolleybus replacement, it was projected over the 698 to Woolwich in 1959 and added a Bexleyheath allocation. Stability followed for the next decade and a half, but in 1977 RMs took over and the Bexleyheath share was removed with the 229's section beyond Erith to create new DMS OMO route 269. At the other end, however, came an extension from Orpington to Farnborough. One-manning swept up the 229 in 1982, at which point its section beyond Green Street Green to Farnborough was lost, and shortly after that, Sidcup replaced its DMSs with Ts. Ms, followed by Ls, also worked from Sidcup in the mid-1980s, but in 1996 the southern section beyond Sidcup Garage was removed to create a Roundabout minibus route. Then came Bexleybus, which in 1988 took on the 229 from a reopened Bexleyheath garage with cream and blue DMSs and Ls. Ts returned when Bexleyheath became part of LBL's London Central subsidiary in 1991, and the 229 was diverted at the southern end to Queen Mary's Hospital. Some old ground was regained in 1994 with an extension to Thamesmead, and stability has returned. PVLs (Volvo B7TLs) replaced the Ts in 2000, WVLs (Volvo B9TLs) replaced the PVLs in 2011, and in 2016 a new operator came in the form of Arriva Kent Thameside, which used new E40Ds based at Dartford. Before 2016 was out, this garage became the responsibility of Arriva London North.

LEFT: On 6 February 2021 at Bexleyheath Broadway Dartford's T 292 (GN61 JRO) is visiting from its normal home on the 160. It was new as Arriva Kent Thameside 6462.

BELOW: Grubby with winter road dirt, T 321 (LK65 EKZ), from the regular allocation of E40Ds, is leaving Erith on the afternoon of 6 February 2021.

230

Upper Walthamstow (Bisterne Avenue), Leyton (Bakers Arms), Walthamstow Central, Blackhorse Road, Tottenham Hale, Turnpike Lane Station, Wood Green Station.

LONDON GENERAL (NP) – BYD DD (Ee)

Just as the 241 had localised the furthest end of the 41, the 230 was introduced in 1973 to split the 241 in half in turn, taking its Manor House–Stratford roads with Leyton RMs. An interesting interlude in 1977 put RTs into action briefly to offset an RM shortage, but in 1981 OMO came with LSs and the diversion of the southern section to Whipps Cross. At the other end, however, it was projected to Finsbury Park. In 1982 another extension took place, from Whipps Cross to Leytonstone. Double-deckers returned in 1987 as Titans, and a simultaneous diversion to Wood Green made the 230 very busy. In 1988 it was diverted via Walthamstow Central and in 1992 via Philip Lane in Tottenham. Low-floor operation came in 1996, accompanying a diversion to untapped Upper Walthamstow, but the Dart SLFs ordered by what was now Stagecoach East London struggled with overcrowding, and neither a PVR upcount nor a new batch of SLDs in 2001 could fix it, so Tridents were rotated in during 2003. In 2013 Arriva London North won the route, using DWs from Tottenham, but lasted only one contract plus time added on; since 2020 London General has had it, using new electric BYDs based at Northumberland Park.

RIGHT: Alexander Dennis's tie-up with Chinese behemoth BYD produced the DD double-decker with Enviro400 City bodywork, which in Go-Ahead parlance is called the Ee class. On 1 July 2020 Ee 31 (LF20 XMJ) is setting off from Wood Green.

BELOW: Northumberland Park's Ee 36 (LF20 XMP) is one stop further along at Wood Green on 20 February 2021.

231

Turnpike Lane Station, Westbury Avenue, Edmonton (Cambridge), Great Cambridge Road, Enfield Town, Enfield Chase Station.

METROLINE (PB) – Alexander Dennis Enviro400 (TE) and Volvo B9TL (VW)

Plying up and down the Great Cambridge Road since 1954, the 231 veered off at Ponders End to reach Forty Hill; this section expanded later to reach Brimsdown and Carterhatch (and even as far onward as Waltham Cross at one point) but in 1998 was withdrawn beyond Enfield Chase. The southern terminal has similarly settled at Turnpike Lane. For many years the responsibility of Enfield garage, under whom it was converted from RT to SMS in 1971 and thence to DMS (1976) and M (1981), it was twinned with the 217 and remained so when both were reallocated to Potters Bar in 1990. DMLs took over in 1998 and TPs in 2003, but between 2007 and 2018 First (London General after 2012) ran it with DNs (later reclassified ENs) from Northumberland Park; since then Potters Bar has returned under Metroline, at first with TEs but now phasing in newer VWs.

LEFT: Volvo B9TL VW 1407 (LK13 BHY), seen at Enfield Town on 24 April 2021, has recently been transferred to Potters Bar to modernise the 231, though its outgoing TEs are mostly of the same vintage.

232

St. Raphael's (Pitfield Way), Neasden, Brent Cross, Finchley, North Circular Road, New Southgate, Arnos Grove, Palmers Green, Wood Green, Turnpike Lane Station.

LONDON GENERAL (NP) – Wrightbus Streetlite (WS)

New in 1994, the 232 was a second go at isolating the 112's eastern section, and this time it stuck. Potters Bar Ms gave way to DLDs (1999) before a rash of garage changes that took the route to Cricklewood (2000), North Wembley (2005), Perivale (2009, with MMs) and back to Cricklewood (2012, with DEs) before its takeover by London General in 2019 with new Streetlites from Northumberland Park.

LEFT: The 232 has a quarter of the North Circular Road to itself, dipping off through Arnos Grove and then getting back on before dropping down at Palmers Green to reach Wood Green and Turnpike Lane. On 20 February 2021 WS 138 (SM19 KKD) is seen in Wood Green.

233

Eltham Station, New Eltham, Longlands Road, Sidcup, Foots Cray, Ruxley Corner, Maidstone Road, Birchwood Corner, Northview Estate, Swanley (Beechenlea Lane).

METROBUS (MB) – Alexander Dennis E20D

A renumbering of the 21A from 1984, the new 233 linked Eltham and Swanley via Avery Hill rather than the 21A's New Eltham routeing. Sidcup Ts (and Ms when they were available, followed by Ls) were in charge, but in 1988 it was lost on tender to Boro'line Maidstone and treated to a mix of blue Leyland Olympians and white Scanias, plus one Volvo Citybus. Kentish Bus acquired Boro'line in 1992 and repainted the buses cream and maroon, running them from Crayford and then Dartford. The Sunday service initially came out of Dartford but was reallocated later to Dunton Green. From 1996 National Greenways in yellow and green were used, but in 1998 Metrobus won the tender and gave it 8.5m Darts in blue and yellow. That company has kept hold of the route ever since in spite of an enforced livery change to red, converting it to Dart SLF in 2003 and to E20D in 2010. Since 1998 the 233 has probed the previously unserved Longlands Avenue in Sidcup, but that was also when the route was rerouted via New Eltham, effectively restoring the old 21A.

RIGHT: Orpington's large collection of disparate mini E20D batches mix indiscriminately on all routes allocated them, including the 233. On 23 August 2020 156 (YX60 FUW) is seen at Sidcup station.

BELOW: On the morning of 24 April 2021 in Eltham High Street, we see 186 (YX13 AJU).

234

Highgate Wood (Sussex Gardens), East Finchley, Muswell Hill Broadway, Coppetts Wood, Friern Barnet, Whetstone, Barnet Church, Barnet (The Spires)

METROLINE (PB) – Alexander Dennis E20D (DEM)

New in 1989, the 234 allowed the lengthy trunk route 134 to fall back to Friern Barnet from the south, and at first followed it all the way to Archway. Potters Bar was in charge with its eclectic collection of second-hand Ms and Vs, but in 1994 the route was converted to minibus with an influx of SRs, necessary to permit rerouteing via Coppetts Wood on its way only as far now as Muswell Hill. For its next contract in 1998, retained by what had become MTL London, new Dart SLFs (DMSs) took over and helped inaugurate an extension from Muswell Hill to East Finchley; at the same time, its garage journeys beyond the border at Barnet to Potters Bar were performed out of service, with the route otherwise standing behind The Spires shopping centre. Metroline purchased MTL later in 1998 but the DMSs stayed put until replacement in 2010 by a mix of longer Dart SLFs (DLDs and DPs) were introduced. A further extension in 2002 took it to Highgate Wood, where there is a turning point. In 2012 a new Metroline contract saw slightly shorter E20Ds purchased, coded DEM, and the members of this original batch have since been joined by incomers from what was previously First.

LEFT: Potters Bar's DEM 1345 (LK62 DDZ) is in Barnet High Street on 31 July 2021.

BELOW: Almost at the other end of the 234 on 31 July 2021 is DEM 1343 (LK62 DDU). This batch of E20Ds was new with black window surrounds, which have since been overpainted in body colour upon mid-career refurbishment.

235

North Brentford Quarter, Brentford, Isleworth, Hounslow, Hounslow Heath, Feltham, Sunbury Cross, Sunbury Village (Three Fishes).

METROLINE (AH) – Alexander Dennis E20D (DEL)

Created in 1996 out of the western end of the 237, the 235 began with Ms from London United's Hounslow garage, but its first tender award gave it to Tellings-Golden Miller in 1998, and white, yellow and blue Dennis Dart SLFs were introduced. London United retained two double-deck workings at school times, first from Hounslow and then Hounslow Heath. In 2000 TGM acquired the western half of Fulwell garage, rechristened it Twickenham and movied in the 235, and for the company's next contract in 2003 took Caetano-bodied Dart SLFs in a predominantly red livery. That year also saw Armchair (soon to be part of Metroline) begin operating the schools double-deckers, though these were separated in 2004 as route 635. TGM itself became part of National Express-owned Travel London and its buses were repainted red, and after a further name change to Abellio in 2009, the next winning contract saw ex-Armchair Darts rotated onto the 235. In 2013 the route was extended to North Brentford Quarter. Metroline won the contract in 2017 and put into service new DEL-class E20Ds, operating them out of Brentford. London United have now won the 235, and will take over in 2022.

RIGHT: Reposing at the 235's Sunbury, Three Fishes stand on 5 April 2021 is Brentford's DEL 2254 (LK66 FSP).

BELOW: Hounslow High Street has been pedestrianised, but three of the many bus routes otherwise bypassing it are allowed in, and one is the 235, personified on 5 April 2021 by DEL 2261 (LK66 FTA).

236

Finsbury Park Station, Highbury Barn, Canonbury, Newington Green, Dalston, Hackney, Homerton Hospital, Kingsmead Estate, Hackney Wick (Eastway).

TOWER TRANSIT (LI) – Wrightbus Streetlite (WV)

The 236 has meandered round inner north London backstreets since 1934, with antecedents for ten years before that. Tottenham and Leyton garages shared it, together converting from LTL to TD and then to RF, but by the 1960s traffic was bedeviling it, so shortening began. 1968 saw it cut back from Leyton to Leytonstone and in 1971 OMO SMSs replaced the crew RFs, Dalston taking over from Tottenham at the same time. LSs appeared in 1978 and remained for a decade, though Dalston closed in 1981 and passed its share of the 236 to Ash Grove. Despite withdrawal between Finsbury Park and Stroud Green in 1982 (at which point Ash Grove came off), almost ridiculous expansion began at the other end, the route being extended to Walthamstow Central in 1987 and the Sunday service then absorbing the 212 on that day to take it all the way to Chingford! This couldn't last, and in 1988 the 236 was split in two, falling back to Hackney Wick. Minibussing followed in 1989 with MRLs from Clapton, and a tendering loss for LBL saw Capital Citybus take over in 1992, with yellow Optare Metroriders from Northumberland Park. These were quickly replaced by Volvo B6s in 1993, by which time a new base at Hackney was in control. In 1998, after First bought Capital Citybus, DMLs took over and in 2012 came DMVs, the longest E20Ds. Tower Transit inherited First's operations in 2013 and four years later introduced new Wrightbus Streetlites.

LEFT: On 16 August 2019 Lea Interchange's WV 46209 (SK17 HGJ) is loading up at Finsbury Park. The garage was opened in 2007 to replace Hackney and passed with the rest of First Capital to Tower Transit in 2013.

BELOW: WV 46204 (SK17 HGC) is coming up to Finsbury Park on 24 April 2021.

237

White City (Bus Station), Shepherd's Bush, Stamford Brook, Turnham Green, Gunnersbury, Kew Bridge, Brentford, Isleworth, Hounslow, Hounslow Heath (Hussar).

METROLINE (AH) – Volvo B9TL (VW)

Long a fixture in the Sunbury area and out beyond to Chertsey, far to the south-west, the 237 eked out a suburban existence with Hounslow-based buses, which between 1953 and 1976 were the bulletproof RFs. Therefore, the last thing anyone expected was for the route to be converted from BL to RM in 1979 and extended over the 117 to Shepherd's Bush. The Sunbury Village–Chertsey leg was lost, but on Saturdays a Turnham Green allocation was added, which passed with that garage's other operations to the new Stamford Brook in 1980. In 1987 it was converted to OPO with Ms and Stamford Brook came off, but this garage took wholesale charge in 1990 with new Ls under a specialised contract, which moved with the privatisation of its operating unit to London United in 1994. Ms returned in 1996, when the 237 was withdrawn between Hounslow Heath and Sunbury Village, and in 1998 the route was transferred on tender to Armchair at Brentford. It has stayed here ever since, though Metroline took over Armchair in 2003, replacing the orange Volvo Olympians with two batches of red Dennis Tridents and then introducing new Volvo B9TLs (VWs) in 2010.

RIGHT: Metroline's VW batch for the 237 and E2 has gone through refurbishment, losing the black accenting to the front panels, as demonstrated by Brentford's VW 1046 (LK10 BXP) at Hounslow on 5 April 2021.

BELOW: A later batch of VWs has since come in, and on 11 April 2019 VW 1215 (LK61 BNN), with revised blinds, is leaving Shepherd's Bush.

238

Stratford (Bus Station), Portway, Plashet Road, Plashet Grove, East Ham, Barking Station.

STAGECOACH EAST LONDON (WH) – Alexander Dennis E40D

Part of a package of trolleybus replacements introduced in 1959, route 238 began as a link between Becontree and North Woolwich via Canning Town; it was shared by Poplar and West Ham with RMs. In 1961 its eastern terminus was revised to Little Heath and in 1965 it was amended at the west to reach Stratford via Plashet Road, becoming daily from West Ham alone. In 1971 it was one-manned with SMSs, Upton Park taking on the Sunday service (with its extension to Chadwell Heath Hospital) later and keeping it until 1975. West Ham now had enough DMSs to double-deck the Sunday service, and in 1977 received more for the weekday service. Another garage change in 1978 reallocated the 238 to Upton Park, with West Ham retained only on Saturdays. Upton Park received Ts in 1981, but the whole route moved again in 1982, pitching up at Barking garage. A localisation programme in 1991 clipped off the service beyond Barking Garage to Little Heath, and in 1993 it was single-decked with DRLs; longer DALs followed in 1995, now under Stagecoach. Titans returned in 1997 and, when reallocated again to Upton Park in 1999, Scanias came onto the 238; Barking retained the Sunday service until 2003. Single-decking was attempted a third time in 2000 with SLD-class Dart SLFs, but this too was overturned with the advent of Tridents in 2003. Upton Park's closure in 2011 restored West Ham garage to control, and not long after came new E40Ds, which have stayed for 2017's Stagecoach East London contract.

LEFT: West Ham's 19852 (LX12 CZF) turns into East Ham High Street on 21 April 2019.

BELOW: 10103 (LX12 DBU), from a later batch of E40Ds despite its lower fleetnumber, is coming into Stratford bus station on 18 April 2019.

240

Golders Green Station, Hendon, Mill Hill East, The Ridgeway, Mill Hill Broadway, Hale Lane, Edgware Station.

METROLINE (EW) – Alexander Dennis Enviro400 (TE)

Long-established in its historic Golders Green-Edgware format, the 240 was a single-deck route with double-deck support as far north as Mill Hill, though it was shared between a myriad of garages including Edgware, Cricklewood and further-away Chalk Farm and Holloway. In 1951 it was standardised on RTs and concentrated at Cricklewood, though between 1959 and 1970 Hendon provied the Sunday service, moving after that to Saturdays. Edgware joined in during 1966. In 1971 OMO came with SMSs into both Edgware and Cricklewood; Metrobuses replaced both allocations in 1980 and restored the upper deck. Cricklewood came off other than on Saturdays in 1983 and altogether in 1985, though Hendon reappeared on Sundays that year and continued until 1986. Ms stayed put on the 240 for over twenty years, though minibuses ran the Sunday service from 1990 until 2001 (DTs, then SRs and then EDRs, once the privatised Metroline had supplanted LBL as the operator). VPL-class Volvo B7TLs took over in 2003, followed in 2012 by TEs (Enviro400s), and these endure today.

RIGHT: New to Brentford for the E2, TE 992 (LK59 DZT) subsequently found its way to Edgware and on 31 August 2018 is coming up to its home base, tucked at the back of Edgware Underground station.

BELOW: On 18 July 2021 at Golders Green, TE 984 (LK59 DZH) is getting going. Only this batch of Enviro400s ever had bumper-mounted marker lights.

241

Stratford City (Bus Station), Stratford, Plaistow, New Barn Street, Freemasons Road, Custom House, Keir Hardie Estate, Canning Town (Hermit Road).

STAGECOACH EAST LONDON (WH) – Alexander Dennis E40D

When it took over from the southern half of the 41 in 1968, new route 241, linking Manor House and the V&A Docks, was RM operated by West Ham. In 1970 its Sunday service was one-manned with SMS and the weekday service followed in 1973, at which time DMSs were introduced. This was when the 241 was withdrawn north of Stratford, new route 230 replacing this section. With the docks moribund, the route was diverted at the southern end to the Kier Hardie Estate, and in 1981 was projected onward to Canning Town. Titans replaced the DMSs in 1982, but the withdrawal of the Kier Hardie Estate-Canning Town leg in 1988 reduced the 241 to a very weak route, which was ripe for minibussing in 1991, with MRLs. Second thoughts restored the service to Canning Town, and in 1992 West Ham closed, passing its buses to Stratford minibus base. Under Stagecoach, Darts phased in, first DWs and then DRLs, before double-deckers returned in 1995 in the form of Upton Park-based Scanias. These gave way to VAs in 1999, when Bow took it over; in 2001 it received low-floor Dennis Tridents and the Sunday Stratford allocation, still with Darts, was transferred to Bow. Stratford gained it back in 2003 and the new West Ham took over in 2008; in 2011 the route was extended to Stratford City. Its latest Stagecoach East London contract, applying from 2018, introduced new Alexander Dennis E40Ds.

LEFT: West Ham's 11023 (YX68 UKH) is turning towards Stratford on the new road layout here.

BELOW: Six E40Ds commonly found on the 241 have LED blinds that can reproduce London Transport's Johnston font; unfortunately, they fritz below 1/60, as demonstrated by 11035 (SN18 KUB) at Stratford on 25 June 2020.

242

Aldgate Station, Commercial Street, Shoreditch, Dalston, Hackney, Powerscroft Road, Clapton Park, Homerton Hospital.

ARRIVA LONDON NORTH (CT) – Volvo B5LH (HV)

Created in 1998 out of fomer route 22B, which itself had been the separated eastern half of the 22, the 242 inherited its predecessor's Leyland Olympians, which underwent repaints out of Kentish Bus livery to become Arriva London North Ls, based at Clapton. Later in the year it hosted the first low-floor double-deckers in the form of DLAs, and although these were replaced in 2003 by newer examples, the class endured on the 242 until 2010, when DWs took over under a renewed Arriva London North contract. Ts and VLWs were also available for use at this point. Unfortunately, successive withdrawals have damaged and then erased the 242's point as a link from east London into the City and West End; in 2017 its contract renewal (with new HVs) was accompanied by a cutback from Tottenham Court Road to St Pauls, and in 2019 the 242 lost its City leg altogether with a rerouteing from Shoreditch to Aldgate. To the north of London there is also the 'real' 242, still extant despite being severed from the London Transport network long ago and its number thus re-used; it still operates from Potters Bar garage, now of Metroline.

RIGHT: Turning left from Dalston Lane into Kingsland High Street on 30 June 2019 is Clapton's HV 241 (LK66 GCV), now able to go no further into town than Aldgate, on the fringes of the City. The cross-London link once offered by the 22 here is now completely gone.

BELOW: HV 242 (LK66 GCX) is at Aldgate, scene of much road alteration in recent years, on 21 March 2021.

243

Wood Green Station, Tottenham, Stamford Hill, Stoke Newington, Dalston, Shoreditch, Old Street, Clerkenwell, Holborn, Aldwych, Waterloo Station.

ARRIVA LONDON NORTH (AR) – Volvo B5LH (HV)

New in 1961, the 243, with Stanford Hill RMs, replaced trolleybus routes 543 and 643, running from Wood Green to Holborn Circus on Mondays to Saturdays; a 243A on Sundays continued on to the London Docks. Wood Green gained an allocation in 1966 and both garages upgraded the 243 to RML in 1970, though Tottenham replaced Wood Green in 1971. Tottenham came off in 1978, returned in 1981 and later in the year supplanted Stamford Hill entirely other than on Saturdays. Stamford Hill's participation ended in 1982 but came back briefly in 1985 when Metrobuses replaced the RMLs as OPO. Stability ensued for the next decade and a half, but in 2000 an important extension was mounted which took the 243 onward from Holborn Circus via withdrawn Red Arrow route 505 to Waterloo. It was also introduced on Sundays and converted from M to DLA daily. DWs replaced the DLAs in 2015 and in 2017, another contract with the incumbent Arriva London North introduced new HV-class Volvo B5LHs.

LEFT: An unusually stable route, with just one major change in its six decades, the 243 by 2018 was operated with hybrid Volvo B5LHs like Tottenham's HV 339 (LF67 EUH), seen approaching Dalston on 18 July 2018.

BELOW: On the morning of 27 March 2021, HV 368 (LF67 EWG) has just crossed Waterloo Bridge to attain the 243's terminus.

244

Woolwich Common (Queen Elizabeth Hospital), Shooters Hill, Woolwich, Plumstead, Broadwaters, Belmarsh Prison, Thamesmead, Abbey Wood Station.

LONDON CENTRAL (BX) – Alexander Dennis E20D (SE)

In 1987 a need was identified for a bus service linking the newly built Broadwaters estate with nearby Woolwich, producing the 244, which worked off the 291 and used its Plumstead Ls. In 1988 this became part of the reopened Bexleyheath garage's Bexleybus network and gained LSs in cream and blue. Optare Metroriders (MRLs) had bedded in by 1991, when the route pushed out beyond Broadwaters to Thamesmead. In 1999 DRLs took over under a renewed London Central contract, under whose terms the 244 was extended from Thamesmead to Abbey Wood. 2000 saw low-floor DMLs introduced, and in 2004 the route became one of those designated to serve the expanded Queen Elizabeth Hospital through an extension from Woolwich via Shooters Hill to approach the new terminus from 'round the back'. The DMLs gave way to transferred LDPs before a new contract in 2011 saw the route reallocated from Bexleyheath to Belvedere and thereby technically become a London General route. SE-class E20Ds took over at this point, and when their term was renewed in 2018, were repainted red. Belvedere closed in 2017 and Bexleyheath resumed control.

RIGHT: Recently repainted out of its original red with grey skirt, Bexleyheath's SE 84 (YX60 FCY) serves the new and much improved arrangements in Woolwich town centre on a drizzly 31 October 2020.

BELOW: On 30 June 2019 SE 62 (YX60 EPO) is over on the other side of Woolwich, near new buildings designed to complement the Crossrail station (when it opens!).

245

Golders Green Station, Cricklewood, Tanfield Avenue, Neasden, Forty Avenue, North Wembley, Sudbury, Sudbury Town Station, Alperton (Sainsbury's).

METROLINE (PV) – Volvo B9TL (VW)

Replacing trolleybus route 645 in 1962, the 245 with its Cricklewood RMs linked North Finchley and Stanmore. Its weekend service was withdrawn in 1964 and in 1968 the remainder was withdrawn between Colindale and Stanmore. Upon its OMO conversion in 1970, its new SMSs were rerouted at Cricklewood to reach Sudbury Town via a withdrawn section of the 16; it was also cut back at the other end to Golders Green, and that form has stayed fixed ever since. It gained a Saturday service at this point but not on Sundays until 1978, when the 245A on that day came off. DMSs operated from 1973 and Ms after 1980, though a need for these and a surfeit of LSs by 1987 obliged conversion to the latter. Ms returned in 1990 and in 1991 the route was reallocated to Harrow Weald garage, though Darts were now in fashion and DTs took over later in the year, working out of North Wembley outstation. In 1992 the 245 was projected from Sudbury Town to Alperton Sainsbury's, this leg becoming daily in 1998 when low-floor DLs were introduced. Dual-door DLDs and later DMLs subsequently became available before the Enviro200 variety of the DML class appeared in 2008 with First's victorious contract, operated out of Alperton. First here was taken over by Metroline West in 2013 and the 245 was soon double-decked with Volvo B9TLs. In 2016 the route was reallocated with its buses from Alperton to Perivale.

LEFT: On 17 July 2021 Perivale's VW 1366 (LK62 DKV) is setting off from Golders Green.

BELOW: On the approaches to Blackbirds Cross on 31 July 2021, VW 1375 (LK62 DNO) is short-working to North Wembley.

246

Bromley North Station, Bromley South, Pickhurst Lane, Hayes Station, Coney Hall, Keston, Leaves Green, Biggin Hill, Westerham Hill, Westerham (Green).

STAGECOACH SELKENT (TB) – Alexander Dennis E20D

Pushing far to the south of the London border, the 246 was introduced in 1998 to replace the Westerham section of the 320 after this route was curtailed at Biggin Hill. Godstone garage of Metrobus operated Darts, and on summer Sundays let them really stretch their legs, with journeys to Chartwell and even Tonbridge. Between 2000 and 2002 a regular service was mounted to East Grinstead. In 2003 new Dart SLFs took over, furnishing an intermediate rerouteing via Hayes, and in 2006 Godstone closed, passing its allocation to Orpington. Then, in 2008, Selkent took over using Dart SLFs from Bromley. 2015 saw Metrobus return, this time with the small number of MAN 12.240s available. Stagecoach Selkent won back the 246 in 2020, using E20Ds but with Bromley just as likely to put out E40D double-deckers.

RIGHT: On 2 May 2021 in Bromley High Street, E20D 36573 (LX13 CZR), new to North Street for the 165 but transferred to Bromley for the 246, is operating its Sunday Chartwell extension.

BELOW: Straying from its rightful 261 on 28 February 2021, but providing extra capacity if anyone fancies it, is E40D 11074 (YX68 UTT) in Bromley High Street.

247

Barkingside Station, Fullwell Cross, Hainault, Hainault Forest, Marks Gate, Collier Row, Romford Station.

STAGECOACH EAST LONDON (NS) – Alexander Dennis E40D

Only obliquely related to the original parent route (withdrawn in 1981 despite being the longest route on the system at 24 miles in length), today's 247 was known as 247A and lost its suffix in 1982. Ts from North Street were in charge, linking Noak Hill (Gidea Park in peaks) and Ilford. In 1986 a peculiar bifurcation was added using the resources (Seven Kings Ts) and routeing of the withdrawn 150; it diverged at Hainault to Chigwell Row. The section beyond Romford was taken off in 1987, together with the North Street allocation other than on Sundays but in 1988 the 150 was resurrected. Seven Kings retained control of the now reduced 247, but North Street regained a share in 1990 and the whole thing in 1993 when Seven Kings closed. This change also saw conversion to Dart (DW) operation and withdrawal between Barkingside and Ilford, though the midibus types used were recycled rapidly as Stagecoach became the privatised operator after 1994; corporate-liveried Volvo B6s and then B10Ms gave way to DRLs and then DALs, with Titans continuing to appear in support. In 1999 SLDs (Dart SLFs) added low-floor capability, but double-deckers returned in 2003 as Dennis Tridents. These lasted the span of two contracts until 2018, when E40Ds were cascaded onto the route.

LEFT: On 13 September 2020 North Street's 19827 (LX11 BLK) is making a typical route 247 journey's final turn from Romford station to the stand not far away.

BELOW: Across the road a few hours earlier in the day gives the possibility of nearside shots for the same manoeuvre, and on 27 March 2021 that's what 19770 (LX11 BFL), with the new Stagecoach logo, is doing.

248

Cranham (Moor Lane), Upminster Park Estate, Avon Road, Upminster Station, Hornchurch, Roneo Corner, Romford Market.

STAGECOACH EAST LONDON (RM) – Scania N230UD

Originally a very short route from Upminster to Cranham, the 248 passed under a low bridge and thus needed single-deckers, though from 1955 it received low-height RLHs and became best known for these much-loved buses, operated by Hornchurch garage. Greater things were lined up for the 248, however, and in 1970 it was one-manned with SMSs and extended westward to Romford. LSs replaced the Swifts but the route was too busy for them and in 1981 Titans were introduced, made possible by clipping the Cranham–Upminster section to avoid the low bridge. Tendering in 1988 wiped out Hornchurch's runout and the 248 was taken over by Frontrunner South East with green Leyland Atlanteans, but this company was soon purchased by Ensignbus and blue buses appeared. Over the next decade, the Dennis Dominators purchased in 1990 became yellow (Capital Citybus) and then red (First Capital). In 2001 the 248 was won by Blue Triangle and Dennis Tridents took over, but this firm lasted just one contract plus two years, and in 2008 East London (in its between-Stagecoach period) won, using new Scanias from Rainham. This contract was retained in 2015 and again in 2020.

RIGHT: During the period of ELBG group ownership, Scanias were preferred over Enviro400s and 175 of them entered service; a decade after Stagecoach's return they are still going, like Rainham's 15015 (LX58 CFE) at Romford on 5 December 2018.

BELOW: 15006 (LX58 CEJ) heads south of Romford on 17 July 2021.

249

Anerley Station, Crystal Palace, Upper Norwood, Streatham Common, Tooting Bec, Balham, Clapham South, Clapham Common Station.

ARRIVA LONDON SOUTH (N) – Volvo B5LH (HV)

More or less identical to the 249 that operated between 1972 and 1989, the 249 of 1991 replaced the 49's southernmost section and used DR-class Darts from Streatham. This garage's closure the following year saw Norwood take over, with an incongruous Sunday service introduced that swallowed up the 349 as well and thus merited double-deckers (Titans from Brixton), though DRs were soon working all week. In 1993 this was amended to reach Sloane Square rather than West Brompton, the 349 having been replaced by a 319 to this point. In 1996, however, the Sunday service was pulled back to the weekday terminus at Tooting Bec. Thornton Heath took over the 249 in 1997, but both this base and Norwood had been bulking out the DRs with whatever else was available, from Ms and Ls to MRs, MRLs and SRs. Permanent double-deck operation was instituted in 1999 with Ls, accompanying reallocation back to Norwood and an extension from Tooting Bec to Balham. At the other end, Crystal Palace bus station became so full that in 2003 the 249 was pushed downhill to Anerley Station. The 249 was the route to usher out the L class in 2005, after which VLAs and DLAs shared it in equal numbers. In 2008 it was extended again, now reaching Clapham Common. 2012 saw London General win, using WVLs from Merton (Stockwell after 2013), though in 2016 the new buses were replaced by elderly PVLs. London General didn't keep the route, and Arriva London South returned in 2017, with HVs from Norwood.

LEFT: Norwood's HV 291 (LK17 AMO) has just made the right turn from Streatham, St Leonard's Church into the High Road on 28 July 2017.

BELOW: HV 395 (LC67 AJX), from a later batch of Volvo B5LHs into Norwood, is passing Crystal Palace on 31 May 2020.

250

West Croydon (Bus Station), London Road, Thornton Heath Pond, Thornton Heath, Green Lane, Streatham, Streatham Hill, Brixton Station.

ARRIVA LONDON SOUTH (TH) – Alexander Dennis Enviro400 (T)

New in 1988 to allow the 159 to fall back from Thornton Heath to Streatham, the 250 continued on to Croydon and was operated by Streatham garage with Ls and Ms. In 1990, however, it passed to Brixton with DMS operation, and later that year Thornton Heath took it over under an LBL tender that specified Ls; a Sunday service was added at that point. After the privatisation of South London and its transformation, via Cowie, into Arriva London South, another contract was won in 1999 and DLAs furnished it. The need to use these temporarily elsewhere during eight months of 2001 saw Brixton take over with Ls, but after that, stability endured, with a night service added. The retained contract in 2010 specified new Enviro400s (Ts) and these continue across the next one, set going in 2017. However, a niggling little change of no benefit to anyone but stand allocators saw the 250 withdrawn between West Croydon and Croydon, Katharine Street in 2019.

RIGHT: On 20 April 2019 Thornton Heath's T 161 (LJ60 AVW), from a later batch of Enviro400s transferred from Tottenham, crosses the Croydon underpass on a section of route since arbitrarily abandoned.

BELOW: Refurbished for the 2017 contract on the 250 and now carrying the new Arriva logos, T 125 (LJ10 HVE) is in Streatham on 31 May 2020, now able to go only as far as West Croydon.

251

Arnos Grove Station, Whetstone, Totteridge, Highwood Hill, Mill Hill Broadway, Watling Avenue, Burnt Oak, Edgware Station.

SOVEREIGN (BT) – Alexander Dennis E20D (DE)

Best known for its unique section through semi-rural Totteridge, the 251 was operated by Palmers Green garage pre-war and Muswell Hill post-war; TDs operated from 1949 and RFs from 1957. In 1963 it was reallocated to Edgware and settled down there, the RFs losing their conductors in 1965. A Sunday extension from Burnt Oak to Edgware was expanded upon with a full-time extension in 1968 beyond that point to Stanmore, and in 1976 the long-established RFs were replaced by BLs, which themselves had a much longer innings than expected, lasting until 1990. DT-class Darts then appeared, with Metroline signwriting, and this LBL subsidiary was privatised in 1994. There was no Sunday service on the 251 between 1982 and 1992, and in 1993 the whole service was withdrawn between Edgware and Stanmore. The DTs gave way to DRs and then SRs, and in 1996 new EDRs, the longest variety of step-entrance Darts, were introduced. These were in turn replaced by DLD-class Dart SLFs, which passed with the route to North Wembley garage in 2004, and in 2007 new MAN 12.240s (MMs) took over. Upon a further reallocation in 2009, Cricklewood was now in charge and used DE-class Enviro200s. Finally, 2011 saw Sovereign take over, using its own variant of DEs from Edgware.

LEFT: On 31 August 2018 DE 20170 (YX11 GCZ) is setting off from Edgware.

BELOW: DE 20197 (YX11 COH) was new in 2011 (as DE 97) and spent its first nine years based at Sovereign's Harrow garage before coming to Edgware in 2020 for the 251 and 326. It is seen in Edgware town centre on 20 July 2020.

252

Hornchurch (Town Centre), Airfield Estate, Elm Park, Roneo Corner, Romford, White Hart Lane, Collier Row Road, Collier Row (Clockhouse Lane).

STAGECOACH EAST LONDON (NS) – Alexander Dennis E40D

Long established in the Collier Row area north of Romford, the 252 initially went to Noak Hill until 1940, but gradually, under the stewardship of Hornchurch garage, began to expand southward; it gained RTs in 1958 and later in the year was extended to South Hornchurch via Elm Park, doubling its runout. That was how it remained for two and a half further decades, gaining SMSs in 1971, DMSs in 1975 and Ts in 1980. When its Titans were needed elsewhere at the end of 1981, LSs stepped in, but the Ts returned in 1982. A Sunday projection to Havering Park introduced in 1974 came off at this time, but in 1984 the 252 was extended from South Hornchurch to Hornchurch to take its current form. The closure of Hornchurch garage after tendering losses in 1988 saw Frontrunner South East take on the 252 with green Leyland Atlanteans, but Ensignbus bought this company a year later and imposed its own blue buses, predominantly Olympians and Metrobuses. Ensignbus became Capital Citybus in 1991 and First Capital in 1998, changing liveries from blue to yellow and then red; Dagenham was always in charge, save for the period of its rebuilding in 2002–05 when Rainham operated it. TNLs (Tridents) appeared for 2001's contract and DNs (Enviro400s) in 2008, but in 2013 Stagecoach East London won and put E40Ds into service from its own Rainham premises, with Scanias also in evidence.

RIGHT: Scania 15001 (LX58 CDV) from Rainham garage is at Hornchurch on 17 July 2021.

BELOW: Pictured south of Romford station on 17 July 2021 is 19829 (LX11 BLV), from the big batches of Enviro400s taken that year after Stagecoach's resumption of control.

253

Hackney Central Station, Clapton, Stamford Hill, Manor House, Finsbury Park, Holloway, Camden Town, Mornington Crescent, Euston Station.

ARRIVA LONDON NORTH (CT) – Wrightbus New Routemaster (LT)

New in 1961 to replace trolleybus route 653 on an inverted U-shaped route linking Tottenham Court Road and Aldgate, the 253 was tremendously busy from the outset and involved participation from most local garages, namely Highgate (known later as Holloway), Edmonton, Stamford Hill, Clapton, Dalston and Ash Grove. RMs remained the staple for its first quarter-century, with occasional help by RMLs and DMs at isolated parts of the week, but in 1987 it was converted to OPO, with Stamford Hill using Ms and Ash Grove Ts. The latter's closure in 1991 saw some of its Ts move to Stamford Hill before their own replacement in 1992 by forty new Ls, not quite enough for the full requirement. A rare structural change saw it pulled back from Warren Street to Mornington Crescent in 1991, but in 1992 it was extended from there to Euston. Stamford Hill closed in 1995 and Clapton took over, but Stamford Hill reopened in 2002 and took a share again until 2003. This was when the 253 was withdrawn between Haackney Central and Aldgate and its Stamford Hill allocation hived off as new route 254; the remainder took DLAs. In 2006 it was the turn of Clapton to close and Stamford Hill regain control, and in 2010 the 253 was upgraded from DLA to VLW operation. HVs took over in 2015 and Borismasters in 2017, and in 2020 yet another garage switch saw Stamford Hill mothballed once again and Clapton resume operation.

LEFT: On 5 April 2019 LT 531 (LTZ 1531), then of Stamford Hill garage, works south through Camden.

BELOW: Now operated by Clapton garage when seen on 13 February 2021, LT 531 (LTZ 1531) is a hundred yards short of its base and the 253's terminus.

254

Aldgate Station, Whitechapel, Mile End Gate, Bethnal Green, Cambridge Heath, Hackney, Clapton, Stamford Hill, Manor House, Finsbury Park, Holloway (Nag's Head).

ARRIVA LONDON NORTH (AE) – Wrightbus New Routemaster (LT)

Splitting the 253 into two had long been on the cards, based on its existing setup as two overlapping sections, but it didn't actually come to pass until the 2003 awards. The resulting new route 254 linked Holloway and Aldgate and was the responsibility of Stamford Hill garage of Arriva London North, with new Volvo B7TLs (VLWs). In 2011 operation was reallocated to Ash Grove, which could add DWs of both types to the mix, and in 2017 the route was selected for conversion to Borismaster operation.

RIGHT: Finsbury Park on 25 February 2018 sees LT 333 (LTZ 1333) coming past, on the last lap of a typical route 254 journey to Holloway.

BELOW: On 2 May 2021 Ash Grove's LT 347 (LTZ 1347) heads south past Bethnal Green station.

255

Balham Station, Weir Road, Radbourne Road, Streatham Hill Station, Streatham, Norbury, Stanford Road, Pollards Hill (Westmorland Way).

ARRIVA LONDON SOUTH (TH) – Alexander Dennis Enviro200 (ENL)

The sixth and current route 255 was introduced in 1998 to clip the top end off the 60, terminating at Clapham Common. Thornton Heath garage of Arriva London South provided DRLs. In 2003, by which time it was LDR-operated, it was diverted at Norbury to give first-time service to Stanford Road. Later that year it was extended from Clapham Common to Stockwell and converted to DDL-class Dart SLFs; DWLs (DAF SB120s) had taken charge by 2008. However, the 255's northern section was attached to the 50 in 2010, resulting in a withdrawal north of Streatham Hill Station. Instead, new ground was identified for it to serve and, after some delays, an extension to Balham was implemented in 2014. In 2017 it was provided with mid-career ENL-class Enviro200s to accompany Arriva London South's contract retention.

LEFT: Thornton Heath's ENL 55 (LJ10 CSV) crosses Streatham, St Leonard's Church junction on 22 May 2021, unfortunately not able to show the destination to Balham in this case.

BELOW: Coming up to Streatham station on 31 May 2020 is ENL 60 (LJ10 CTF). This bus was new to Barking for the 173, but came south when that route was double-decked.

256

Noak Hill (Tees Drive), Noak Hill Road, Hilldene Avenue, Harold Hill, Harold Wood, Ardleigh Green Road, Emerson Park, Hornchurch, Hornchurch (St. George's Hospital).

STAGECOACH EAST LONDON (NS) – Alexander Dennis E40D

New in 1988 as a St George's Hospital-Noak Hill minibus link, it was the only one of its tender tranche to be retained by LBL and thus came to North Street garage, with Hornchurch closed. MCW Metroriders (MRs) commenced it, but the contract was for only two years and County Bus won it next, using Mercedes-Benz 709Ds from 1990. This company would hold on to the 256 for the next two decades, becoming part of Arriva Southend. In 1996 the route was extended to Harold Hill and the next two generations of buses were Dennis Darts (1996) and DAF SB120s (2002). In 2013, however, Stagecoach East London won the 256 and put into service new E20Ds from Rainham garage, plus one double-deck working with an E40D. In 2021, as a side-effect of the COVID pandemic, it was double-decked throughout.

RIGHT: Now settled in on route 256 when sighted just to the north of Hornchurch on 17 July 2021 is Rainham's 19792 (LX11 BHK).

BELOW: 19830 (LX11 BLZ) is pulling into the small bus stand at Harold Wood station on the morning of 17 July 2021.

257

Stratford (Bus Station), Maryland, Leytonstone High Road, Green Man Roundabout, Whipps Cross, Leyton (Bakers Arms), Walthamstow Central Station.

STAGECOACH EAST LONDON (T) – Alexander Dennis E40D and E40H

Every cross-Stratford north-south route has ended up being sectionalised sooner or later, and the 262 was no exception, giving its Stratford-Chingford Mount end to new route 257 in 1988. West Ham garage had it with Titans but quickly passed it along to Leyton. There was a shortlived extension to Chingford Mount Fantaseas for the duration of this attraction's being open (1990–92). Later in 1992 Capital Citybus took over with second-hand Dennis Dominators, operated out of Northumberland Park and then, in 1996, from Hackney. The unwise decision was made in 2001 to single-deck the 257, gambling that the low-floor Dart SLFs (DMLs) used would make up for this, but they struggled desperately and new Tridents (TNLs) were ordered to replace them within a year. In 2005 the route was won by Stagecoach East London and put into Stratford with new Dennis Tridents; West Ham took over in 2008, but in 2012 Northumberland Park came back, now under London General following Go-Ahead's purchase of this part of First, and 05-reg Volvo B7TLs (WVLs) were used. These lasted for one contract and two years on top, after which Stagecoach won it back. Leyton now find themselves in charge, using a mix of cascaded 62-reg E40Ds and a handful of new 67-reg MMC E40Hs to support them.

LEFT: Delivered for the 257's contracted proportion of new hybrid buses, Leyton's 12429 (YX67 VBF) leaves Walthamstow Central on 11 March 2020.

BELOW: Not one of the 257's transferred E40Ds, but already at Leyton for the 275, 10123 (LX12 DDV) in Hoe Street on 13 February 2021 has retained part of the branding for that route in its front upper-deck window.

258

Watford Junction, Bushey, Bushey Heath, Harrow Weald, Wealdstone, Harrow, Harrow School, Roxeth, South Harrow Station.

SOVEREIGN (BT) – Alexander Dennis E40D (ADE) and E40H (ADH)

A localisation of the 182's short-lived leg out beyond the border to Watford Junction, the 258 began in 1970 with four Harrow Weald MBs. In 1976 SMSs replaced the MBs and, a little later, an extension past Harrow to South Harrow was mounted. LSs appeared in 1979 and by 1984 enough Ms were spare on Saturdays to double-deck the route on that day of the week. As part of the Harrow Buses network from 1987, the 258's buses became red and cream and the route was diverted via Harrow School to replace the 136. Harrow Weald was hit hard when the next round of tenders came in during 1990, and the 258 thus passed to Luton & Dstrict in 1991, usng new green Darts from Garston. This company lasted just the five years of this particular contract and in 1996 London Buslines took over, with yellow Darts. After First absorbed London Buslines, head office transferred it to its existing Centrewest subsidiary at Alperton garage, and in 2001 the contract awarded to this company introduced new TN-class Tridents. However, Garston returned in 2006, now as an Arriva the Shires garage, and kept hold of it on the next tender as well, using DAF DB250RS(LF)s. Garston was transferred to Arriva London North in 2016 and run down; the 258's loss to Sovereign in 2017 provided the excuse needed to close it. Edgware garage now provides E40Ds, with a smattering of new MMC E40Hs.

RIGHT: On 31 August 2018 ADE 40407 (YX12 FNN), new to London United at Hounslow, is seen in Harrow town centre.

BELOW: Edgware's ADE 40418 (YX12 FOA) is about to make the right turn towards Harrow station on 20 July 2020.

259

King's Cross (Gray's Inn Road), Caledonian Road, Holloway, Finsbury Park, Manor House, Seven Sisters, Tottenham, Edmonton Green Station.

ARRIVA LONDON NORTH (AR) – Volvo B5LH (HV)

Replacing trolleybus 659 in 1961, the 259 began as a Holborn Circus–Lower Edmonton service with RMs from Highgate and Wood Green garages, though Tottenham replaced Wood Green in 1962. On Sundays it continued on to Waltham Cross until 1966, when the Sunday service came off altogether. Tottenham took sole charge from 1971 but Edmonton was back by the time DMS OMO was introduced in 1973. Both garages converted to M in 1982 and Edmonton withdrew shortly after, only to come back briefly in 1985, lasting eight months before its closure, at which point Enfield was given a share. During 1985 the 259 was extended northwards to Hammond Street daily to replace the 279, but lost this section in 1987, plus, oddly, the whole service on Saturdays. It was withdrawn on Sundays again in 1988. A more standard daily format was restored in 1992 when it was used to replace the 221's section into town, but in 1998, when it was awarded on tender to Capital Citybus, the route was standardised between Edmonton Green (Lower Edmonton as was) and King's Cross. Northumberland Park used Metrobuses until its Dennis Arrows were delivered, then replaced them in 2003 with Volvo B7TLs; under London General ownership from 2013, these VNLs were reclassified WVNs. Arriva London North returned to the 259 in 2017 with new Volvo B5LHs (HVs) from Tottenham.

LEFT: At Tottenham on 21 April 2019, HV 217 (LK66 HDE) has just come through the recently-constructed bus-only southbound lane.

BELOW: Tottenham's HV 221 (LJ17 WVF) is nearly at the end of a journey to King's Cross on 31 August 2018.

260

White City (Bus Station), Shepherd's Bush, East Acton, North Acton, Park Royal (Asda), Central Middlesex Hospital, Harlesden, Willesden, Cricklewood, Golders Green Station.

METROLINE (AC) – Volvo B5LH (VWH)

New in 1962, the 260 replaced trolleybus route 660 and began with RMs from Finchley and Stonebridge. Hendon helped on Sundays but soon withdrew and Cricklewood appeared instead. There existed for some years a Sunday extension over the 26 beyond Barnet Church to Chesterfield Road, which remained even as withdrawals in 1971 cut the route back from Hammersmith to a basic North Finchley-Willesden Garage format, with peak runs as far as Acton Vale. By 1973 it was operated by three garages on different days of the week, but was simplified in 1978 with restoration to Hammersmith and apportionment between Willesden and Stonebridge garages. The latter closed in 1981 and cutbacks resumed, 1984 seeing the Willesden Garage-Hammersmith section removed altogether and crew Ms introduced in preparation for OPO, which ensued in 1985. Still, a more important objective was secured in 1987 when the 260 was extended to Shepherd's Bush Green over the short-lived 255, an outgrowth of the 12. Between 1990 and 1998 Armchair were in charge, with orange and white Leyland Olympians, before Willesden returned with Ms as a Metroline garage. AV-class Volvo Olympians followed and were themselves supplanted by VP-class Volvo B7TLs in 2003, when the northern end was clipped this time, terminating at Golders Green. Stability has been the watchword ever since, with Metroline retaining the contract in 2010 and 2017 and using new VWH-class Volvo B5LHs with the latter one.

RIGHT: On 15 September 2020 Willesden's VWH 2314 (LK17 DFN) leaves the Shepherd's Bush end of White City bus station, the 260's terminus since 2008.

BELOW: The morning of 21 April 2019 sees VWH 2378 (LK67 EKT) serving Westfield, opposite Shepherd's Bush station.

261

Lewisham (Town Centre), Lee Green, Grove Park, Bromley, Bromley Common, Locksbottom, Princess Royal University Hospital.

STAGECOACH SELKENT (TB) – Alexander Dennis E40D

Fashioned out of Bromley garage's half of former south-east London fixture 94 in 1982, the 261 on its way between Lewisham and Orpington passed its operating garage, unlike its predecessor. RMs were in charge, but OMO was quickly instituted and a side-effect was that Bromley was only able to field LSs until the last of the Titan production run was made available at the end of 1984 to restore the upper deck. The inherited Saturday run beyond Lewisham to Brockley Rise lasted until 1985. The following year, however, saw the 261's Bromley Common–Orpington section clipped off to form a Roundabout minibus route; and in 1987 it was awarded under tender to Metrobus, who managed to hold on to it for the next quarter-century. Metrobus acquired second-hand Leyland Olympians, replacing them in 1997 with new Volvo Olympians and in 2002 with Dennis Tridents, which lasted until 2009 when East Lancs Omnidekka-bodied Scanias took over. The route itself had expanded again during this time, serving the Princess Royal Hospital from 2007. In 2013 Stagecoach Selkent won the 261 and introduced new Alexander Dennis E40Ds; its successful defence of the contract five years later was predicated on the order of new MMC E40Ds.

LEFT: Bromley's 11071 (YX68 UTO) swings into the still-trafficable section of Bromley High Street on 2 May 2021.

BELOW: On 28 February 2021, just up the street, 11067 (YX68 UTK) is heading in the opposite direction.

262

Stratford (Bus Station), Plaistow, Prince Regent Lane, Tollgate Road, Beckton, Cyprus, Gallions Reach, East Beckton (Sainsbury's).

TOWER TRANSIT (LI) – Wrightbus Streetdeck (WH)

New in 1966 to replace the old 26 between Stratford and Leyton, it came into its own in 1968 with extensions north and south; it now linked Chingford and the V&A Docks, and West Ham garage joined Leyton, both with RMLs. In 1972 West Ham's share was converted to RM, and on Sundays both garages put OMO DMSs into action. Now a little long, the 262 lost its Walthamstow Central-Chingford section (and Leyton allocation) in 1973 and in 1978 was converted to DM operation, though RMs returned a year later. Leyton continued on Saturdays until 1981, when OMO came throughout, with DMSs. Ts took over in 1982. With the redevelopment of Docklands, the 262 was rerouted to East Beckton in 1986 and its Sunday service replaced by a 262A. Then in 1988 came withdrawal north of Stratford, though the southern end was extended on to Canning Town, lasting until 1991. West Ham closed in 1992 and Upton Park now stepped up, its Scanias (Ss) eventually outnumbering the Titans there. On Sundays from 1993 the 262 returned on Sundays with Stratford minibuses (first RBs and SRs, then DWs before double-decking and reallocation to Upton Park in 1995). VN-class Volvo Olympians appeared in 1997 to accompany an extension to Showcase Cinema (until 2008), but reallocation to Bow in 1999 saw the VA variant instead. Then came 9.9m Tridents in 2003. Contract renewal in 2014 saw Scanias predominate and this continued until 2019 when Tower Transit won the contract. Lea Interchange used VN-class Volvo B9TLs for the first year before Wrightbus Streetdecks (WHs) were made available.

RIGHT: Lea Interchange's WH 31104 (SN68 AGA) was always intended for the 262 and 473 but spent its first year on the 25 until that route's loss to Stagecoach. It is seen at Beckton on 27 March 2021.

BELOW: At the other end of the 262, WH 31108 (SK19 FDL) is coming into Stratford on 17 April 2021.

263

Highbury Barn, Highbury, Holloway, Archway, Highgate Station, East Finchley, North Finchley, Whetstone, Barnet Church, Barnet Hospital.

METROLINE (PB) – Alexander Dennis Enviro400 (TE)

New in 1971, the 263 was introduced to take the topmost ends off former routes 17 and 104, and was operated by Finchley garage RMs with Holloway participating at weekends, when it was extended beyond Archway to King's Cross and Farringdon Street. DMS OMO came in 1972, Finchley upgrading to Ms in 1980, but in 1983 both were removed, plus everything south of Archway; Potters Bar garage took charge with Ms, furnishing an extension to Potters Bar Station. In the late 1980s all sorts of second-hand-vehicles prevailed, but in 1989 nine new Scanias modernised the route. As the terminus lay beyond the London border, the 263 was withdrawn north of Barnet in 1994, despite the continuing need to run dead to the garage. In 1996 the route passed to Cowie Leaside, with Wood Green garage operating new DAF DB250s. What was by 2001 Arriva London North then sub-contracted the 263 to First Capital due to staff shortages and Northumberland Park ran yellow and red Volvo Olympians for a year, after which Potters Bar returned, now as a Metroline London Northern route with new TAs. It was reallocated to Holloway in 2003 with TPs but returned to Potters Bar in 2004; TEs furnished the 2009 contract, which featured an extension from Archway to Holloway. It was further projected to Highbury Barn in 2014. During the first four months of 2021, a Holloway allocation was added but then withdrawn again.

LEFT: Having reached Highbury & Islington station from the north-west on 17 December 2019, Potters Bar's TE 922 (LK58 KFY) will have to head north again to reach the 263's Highbury Barn stand.

BELOW: Newer E40Ds can also work the 263, like freshly-repainted TE 1428 (LK62 DYD) at Highbury on 17 July 2021.

264

West Croydon (Bus Station), Mitcham Common, Mitcham, Tooting Broadway, Tooting (St. George's Hospital).

ARRIVA LONDON SOUTH (TC) – Wrightbus Gemini 2 (DW)

It was fortuitous that the number 264 happened to be vacant when it came time to sectionalise the 64's Tooting-Croydon section in 1987; it began with Merton DMSs on Mondays to Saturdays and Croydon DMSs and Ls on Sundays. In 1988 Thornton Heath took over and in 1990 upgraded to Ls under contract. Its Sunday extension over the 64 to New Addington came off at the same time. The Ls were assisted by DMSs, then Ts and finally Ms before another transfer took place in 1998, this time to Croydon with Ms and Ls. This didn't last long, Thornton Heath taking back the 264 in 1999, though Croydon returned on Sundays in 2000. In 2001 the route was reallocated to Beddington Farm, and in 2003 it received DWs to fulfil a contract retained by Arriva London South. Beddington Farm closed in 2012 and Croydon resumed control, and by the end of the decade the 264's complement had advanced from the DAF DB250RS(LF) variant of the DW class to the Wrightbus Gemini 2s wearing higher stock numbers of the same code. Ts (Enviro400s and E40Ds) also assist in strength.

RIGHT: On 7 July 2019 we see Croydon's DW 508 (LJ62 BDO) at Tooting Broadway, on the last leg of a typical route 264 journey to St George's Hospital.

BELOW: E40D T 285 (LJ13 CGG), bought for the 60, has been capable of working on the 264 ever since it was new, and on 31 May 2020 it is doing just that at Tooting Broadway.

265

Putney Bridge Station, Putney Common, Roehampton Lane, Queen Mary's Hospital, Alton East Estate, Roehampton Vale, Kingston Vale, New Malden, Tolworth (Red Lion).

LONDON UNITED (TV) – Alexander Dennis E20D (DLE)

When introduced in 1984, the 265's two new Putney Ms provided a direct link to Queen Mary's Hospital round a unidirectional loop, but this was amended in 1985 to go via unserved Mill Hill East beyond Putney Common. In 1991 it was converted to MA minibus and extended over the 72 to Tolworth Broadway, and during the 1990s upgraded successively to DRs and then DRLs, with short-lived help from the unhappy ML class of Marshall Minibuses and finally DMS-class Dart SLFs. In 2002 it was won on tender by London United and furnished with new Dart SLFs (DPSs) from Tolworth garage, where it has remained ever since. 2016's contract renewal saw new E20Ds arrive, but they were classified in the DE series meant for shorter versions and only recently have assumed final numbers in the DLE class.

LEFT: On a sunny 31 May 2021 DLE 30134 (LJ16 EXT) is coming into Putney Bridge Station Approach. It spent its first four years under the identity of DE 20134.

BELOW: Tolworth's DLE 30129 (LJ16 EXL) speeds through New Malden on 5 April 2021, serving the 265's dogleg off the A3. When new, this MMC E20D was known as DE 20129.

266

Acton (Old Town Hall), Horn Lane, Gypsy Corner, North Acton, Harlesden, Willesden, Cricklewood, Staples Corner, Brent Cross Shopping Centre.

LONDON UNITED (RP) – Alexander Dennis E40D (ADE) and E40H (ADH)

Introduced in 1962 to take over from trolleybus route 666, the 266 linked Edgware and Hammersmith with RMs from Stonebridge and Cricklewood garages. In 1968 Willesden replaced Stonebridge and 1970 saw the route cut back to West Hendon, or Colindale in the peaks. From 1972 Riverside and Cricklewood shared operaion on Mondays to Saturdays, with Stonebridge and Willesden on Sundays (and with RMLs from 1975). The opening of Brent Cross in 1976 provided an important new terminus, although the peak-hour leg to Colindale remained and in 1978 was extended to Mill Hill Broadway. Willesden garage withdrew in 1978 and Stonebridge replaced its RMs with DMs and then crew Ms before closing in 1981 and permitting the return of Willesden on Sundays; the Mill Hill leg finished at this time. in 1982 Cricklewood assumed sole control of the 266, converting from RM to crew M in 1984 and then OPO in 1985. Willesden came back again to assist and in 1990 took over wholly. Garage changes after the privatisation of Metroline restored Cricklewood (1998) and added Harlesden (2000), with the route now converted from M to AV operation. A new Metroline contract in 2005 put the route back into Cricklewood with new Dennis Tridents (TAs), but in 2012 First won and began operating the 266 out of Atlas Road with VNs (Volvo B9TLs). First gave way to Tower Transit in 2013 and reallocated the route to Westbourne Park in 2017, but back came Metroline in 2019 with Cricklewood TEs. This was a short-term contract and in 2019 London United took over, Park Royal operating ADEs and ADHs on a 266 curtailed to Acton.

RIGHT: Coming through Harlesden on 10 December 2019 is Park Royal's ADE 40468 (YX62 BPU), new to the 220 but now available for the 266 as well.

BELOW: Hybrid E40H ADH 45040 (YX62 FOA) is also in Harlesden, but on 12 June 2021 is going the other way.

267

Hammersmith (Bus Station), Stamford Brook, Turnham Green, Gunnersbury, Kew Bridge, Brentford, Isleworth, Twickenham, Fulwell (South Road).

ABELLIO (TF) – Wrightbus New Routemaster (LT)

New in 1962 to replace trolleybus route 667, the 267 had many roads to itself and stable vehicle eras, operating RMs until 1971, DMSs until 1979 and Ms all the way to 2002, all from Fulwell with Turnham Green in assistance between 1971 and 1986. The Fulwell-Hampton Court section was clipped off in 1991 but continued through on Sundays until 2011. After the Ms left, TAs operated, themselves to be replaced by SLEs in 2006 and SPs in 2008. The very last of the Borismasters were allocated across the cusp of 2017/18, and in the ownership of TfL transferred across the garage wall to Abellio when that company won the 267 in 2019.

LEFT: LT 995 (LTZ 2195) was one of the last Borismaster deliveries, beginning at Fulwell of London United but transferring to neighbouring Abellio. It is seen approaching Hammersmith on 25 May 2021.

268

Golders Green Station, Hampstead Heath, Hampstead, Rosslyn Hill, Belsize Avenue, Swiss Cottage, Finchley Road (Sainsbury's).

METROLINE (W) – Alexander Dennis Enviro200 (DE)

Always the unique link across the top of Hampstead Heath, the 268 since introduction in 1968 fielded MBs (1968), SMs (1976), SMDs (1977) and LSs (1978). Tendering took it to London Country North West (1986), R&I (1989), MTL London (1994) and Metroline (1998), with multiple garage changes here until 2006, when Arriva the Shires took over with DAF SB120s (DWLs) from Garston. Metroline returned in 2018 with Cricklewood DEs.

LEFT: On a sunny 17 July 2021 Cricklewood's DE 1128 (LK10 BYU) is coming up to Golders Green station at the end of a typical journey over the top of Hampstead Heath on the 268.

269

Bexleyheath (Shopping Centre), Bexley, Hurst Road, Faraday Avenue, Sidcup, Queen Mary's Hospital, Perry Street, Chislehurst, Bickley, Bromley North Station.

ARRIVA LONDON NORTH (DT) – Wrightbus Gemini 2 (DW)

This route began in 1977 as a sectionalisaton of the Woolwich–Sidcup end of the 229 but has wandered away from those beginnings. Its Bexleyheath-operated DMSs gave way to Titans in 1983, and in 1985 its extension from Sidcup to Bromley North formed the basis of the modern route. Bexleyheath garage's closure in 1986 meant the transfer of the 269 to Plumstead with Ls, but when Bexleyheath reopened in 1988 it returned and now assumed LS operation in blue and cream livery, accompanied by withdrawal between Bexleyheath and Woolwich. Bexleybus lost its entire portfolio on retender, resulting in the 269's takeover in 1991 by Kentish Bus, with cream and maroon Leyland Olympians brought down from Northumbria to work out of Northfleet. When Volvo Olympians came available from the surrender of the 161 at the end of 1995, these took over the 269 and gained Arriva livery in 1998, just in time for the 269 to be lost to Stagecoach Selkent. Plumstead resumed operation, now with SLD-class Dart SLFs, but double-deckers returned in the form of Tridents for the company's 2004 contract. Two complete terms later, with two years on top of each, the 269 was retendered and this time Arriva London North, heirs to Kentish Bus, won, with DW operation out of Dartford.

RIGHT: Bexleyheath town centre is the location for a winter-grubby DW 440 (LJ11 ABZ) on 6 February 2021.

BELOW: Leaving Bromley North on 30 August 2019 is Dartford's DW 426 (LJ61 CEO), with DW 444 (LJ11 AAE) on stand behind it.

270

Putney Bridge Station, Putney Bridge Road, Wandsworth, Earlsfield, Tooting Broadway, Mitcham (Commonside West).

ABELLIO (BC) – Alexander Dennis E40H

New in 1985, the 270 linked up the southern end of the 220 with the northern end of the 280, two routes that had otherwise grown a little long for contemporary traffic conditions. It operated Ms from Merton until low-floor Volvo B7TLs of PVL class arrived in 2000, and when their time in turn was up, in came a mix of mid-life WVLs and Es, plus lone Wrightbus WSD 1. These weren't enough for London General to hold on to the contract, however, and in 2020 the 270 was awarded to Abellio for operation from Beddington Cross. New E40Hs were specified, though their delivery was held up by the pandemic-induced factory shutdown.

LEFT: 2023 (SK20 AZN) is just north of Tooting Broadway in the late afternoon of 30 July 2020.

BELOW: On the morning of 31 May 2020, 2025 (SK20 AZP) of Beddington Cross heads through a locked-down Tooting.

271

Highgate Village (South Grove), Archway, Holloway, Highbury, Canonbury Road, Hoxton, Old Street Station, Moorgate (Finsbury Square).

METROLINE (HT) – Volvo B5LH (VWH)

Directly replacing trolleybus route 611 in 1960, the 271 began with fifteen Highgate RMs, though during the 1960s there was an interlude with XAs and then RMLs before OMO came in 1971 with DMSs; the garage was known as Holloway by this point. Metrobuses followed in 1984, and in 1990, when reallocation to Chalk Farm was implemented, Titans took over. Chalk Farm's closure in 1993 restored Holloway Ms, but in the same year London Suburban Buses took over with a mix of Titans and Volvo Olympians. MTL London's acquisition of this company in 1995 saw the 271 restored to Holloway the following year and all was as it had been, with the Vs supported by returning Ms. In 2003 TPs replaced the Vs and since then the route has fielded TPs, VPs, TPLs, TEs and TEHs in whichever proportions were held by Holloway, until today's newish VWH-class Volvo B5LHs. The southern terminus at weekends has been Liverpool Street off and on, the latest curtailment at the traditional Moorgate stand being due to Crossrail construction.

RIGHT: The 271 has been in the second tier of Holloway routes ever since coming back from London Suburban Buses, but the sheer numbers of VWHs now based permit more stability. Many are the updated variant, like VWH 2310 (LK17 DFF) ascending Highgate Hill on 17 July 2021.

BELOW: VWH 2015 (LK14 FBL) is at Archway on 17 July 2021; this bus was new to the 7 at Perivale West.

272

Chiswick (Grove Park), Sutton Court Road, Turnham Green, Emlyn Road, East Acton, Du Cane Road, White City, Shepherd's Bush Green.

LONDON UNITED (V) – Alexander Dennis E40D (DLE)

New in 2002, this Stamford Brook DR-operated London United contract replaced part of the H40, but plans to extend it through Chiswick to Strand-on-the-Green met with locals' resistance, though similar opposition to the buses' passing along Emlyn and Larden Roads in the back of Acton was faced down. DPK-class Dart SLFs formed the basis of the 202 contract, but upon retender in 2007 NCP Challenger won it, using new short Enviro200s (ADSs). In 2009 this company was first renamed NSL Services and then bought by London United, though the Park Royal base was retained. The ADSs became SDEs and migrated with the route to Shepherd's Bush garage in 2012. In 2017 it was further reallocated to Stamford Brook, and for its successful retention by London United in 2019 it was replenished with new E20Ds (DMEs, though the longer DLEs have since gained prominence).

LEFT: On 12 December 2020 Stamford Brook's DLE 30345 (YX68 UWK) works a 272 through Acton Vale.

BELOW: Passing the Shepherd's Bush end of the Westfield complex on 17 July 2021 is DLE 30343 (YX68 UWH).

273

Lewisham (Tesco), Lee, Burnt Ash Hill, Horn Park, Grove Park, Dunkery Road, Chislehurst, Leesons Hill, St. Mary Cray, Poverest Road, Petts Wood Station.

STAGECOACH SELKENT (TL) – Alexander Dennis E20D

The 273 is actually a second try at a Lewisham–Horn Park backstreet link that originally lasted from 1989 to 1991; the iteration of 1994 along much the same roads stuck this time, with Catford minibuses once again in charge. In 1995 it was extended to Grove Park and in 1997 received new MW-class Varios, but in 2001 greater things beckoned when it was projected on from here to Petts Wood to replace a section that had never really settled with anything, from 161 to 161A to 162. In 2002 it was tendered and awarded to First, who set it going with Darts (DWs) from Orpington before new low-floor Dart SLFs (DMSs) were delivered. Five years later Selkent took it back to Catford, with new Enviro200s; this company returned to Stagecoach ownership in 2010 and kept hold of the 273, with its latest complement being 66-reg E20Ds. A rerouteing the long way through St Mary Cray to and from Petts Wood when a key junction was out of action proved so popular that it was adopted permanently.

RIGHT: Catford's 36624 (SN66 WMV), an 8.9m E20D, is seen drawing up to Lewisham on 25 April 2017 when new. The 273 is considerably longer now than when it was introduced (or reintroduced, in fact, there having been a predecessor of the same number over the same streets).

BELOW: Setting off from Lewisham in the southbound direction on 17 April 2021 is 36630 (SN66 WNB).

274

Islington (Angel), Copenhagen Street, Caledonian Road, Agar Grove, Camden Town, London Zoo, Prince Albert Road, Baker Street, Marble Arch, Lancaster Gate.

METROLINE (KC) – Volvo B5LH (VMH)

With the 74's diversion away from its time-honoured Camden Town terminus to King's Cross in 1991, new route 274 was introduced to fill the gap, terminating at Marble Arch. Chalk Farm was in control, first with Ts, then with DRL-class Darts a year later, but in 1993 this garage closed and Holloway took over; in 1994 this garage was privatised with MTL London Northern (from 1998 part of Metroline). In 1997 the 274 was extended from Camden Town over unserved roads to the Angel, and in 2001 new low-floor Dart SLFs (DLDs) came. Reallocation to the new King's Cross garage ensued in 2003, shortly after a short extension from the overcrowded set of stands at Marble Arch to Lancaster Gate, and DE-class Enviro200s followed in 2011, by which time a second base at King's Cross had been taken. For the 274's successful contract defence in 2018, Metroline converted it back to double-deck with new MCV-bodied Volvo B5LHs, though they had to wait until there had been some tree pruning on roads that had never seen double-deckers.

LEFT: On 21 March 2021 King's Cross-based VMH 2460 (LK18 AKX) heads south past Baker Street station.

BELOW: VMH 2487 (LK18 AHV) is coming round Marble Arch on 17 February 2019.

275

St. James Street Station, Walthamstow Central, Highams Park Station, Woodford Green, Woodford Bridge, Fullwell Cross, Barkingside (Tesco).

STAGECOACH EAST LONDON (T) – Alexander Dennis E40D

Picking across the top of the London bus map ever since its introduction in 1960 to replace trolleybus route 675, the 275 began with Walthamstow RMs and a Wood Green-Enfield Town remit. However, the Reshaping Plan of 1968 saw it hacked unceremoniously in half, diverted at the west to Walthamstow Central Station and converted to MB OMO as one of the designated feeder shuttles. It did grow at the other end, however, being extended to Claybury Hospital in 1971 and to Barkingside in 1977. DMSs came in 1975 and Titans in 1981, though the need to provide Titans for the 48 in 1985 obliged its reallocation to Leyton and demotion to LS. Tendering took it away quickly, Eastern National assuming control in 1986 with its own Leyland Nationals; this company was renamed Thamesway in 1990 but struggled with reliability and Grey-Green took over in 1992, restoring double-decks in the form of miscellaneous Scanias and Volvo Citybuses from Barking garage. This company continued on, becoming Arriva London North-East in 1998 and turning its buses red. In 2005 VLW-class Volvo B7TLs were introduced, but 2012 saw Stagecoach East London win the tender and Leyton came back, this time with Dennis Tridents. E40Ds comprised the next generation and continue today.

RIGHT: On 21 April 2019 Essex-registered 10160 (EU62 AZO) leaves Walthamstow Central. This bus came for the 257, but there is a large E40D allocation at Leyton garage so is bound to wander.

BELOW: Leyton's 10155 (EU62 AXT) swings off Hoe Street towards Walthamstow Central on 25 June 2020.

276

Newham Hospital, Prince Regent Lane, Canning Town, Stratford, Bow Church, Old Ford, Hackney Wick, Homerton Hospital, Hackney Downs, Stoke Newington.

DOCKLANDS BUSES (SI) – Alexander Dennis E20D (SE)

Replacing the old 278's third distinctive routeing, the 276 upon its 1984 debut linked Stoke Newington and Canning Town with LSs from Poplar garage. A year later it was reallocated to West Ham and extended to East Beckton, though it was ahead of its time in this developing area and in 1988 was diverted to North Woolwich instead. Minibuses (RBs and SRs) followed upon its reallocation to Bow in 1990 and Stratford garage took these on in 1992. The East Beckton leg was restored in 1993, and Metroriders had replaced the Renaults by the time Stagecoach East London was formed out of this London Buses Ltd subsidiary in 1994. DW-class Darts came next, in 1995 and SLDs (Dart SLFs) in 1998. In 1999 the 276 was withdrawn between Newham General Hospital and East Beckton, and in 2007 the closure of Carpenters Road for Olympics construction obliged a rerouteing via Wick Lane. Thus did Stratford garage have to close, and a new West Ham took over in 2008. Longer Dart SLFs replaced the original ones and for a time they were supported by Optare Tempo hybrids. However, Stagecoach lost the 276 to Docklands Buses in 2011, and this company put into action new E20Ds from Silvertown garage; these continue today.

LEFT: The pedestrianisation of the Narroway at Hackney has resulted in an awkward diversion of southbound buses, being performed by Silvertown's SE 126 (YX61 BXB) on 13 February 2021.

BELOW: Coming into Stratford bus station on 17 April 2021 is SE 137 (YX61 BWN).

277

Dalston Junction, Hackney, Well Street, Victoria Park, Mile End, Limehouse, Canary Wharf, Westferry Road, East Ferry Road, Crossharbour (Asda).

STAGECOACH EAST LONDON (WH) – Alexander Dennis E40H

New in 1959 to replace trolleybus route 677, the 277, with Clapton RTLs, linked Smithfield and Cubitt Town. 1961 brought it a Sunday extension to Poplar and this was added on Saturdays in 1964 with a Poplar RTL allocation on that day. RTs took over in 1967, Poplar following suit in 1968 and adding a Sunday share. The extension to Poplar was rendered daily in 1969 and Poplar garage's allocation was revised to Mondays to Saturdays. DMS OMO came in 1974 but the buses couldn't work beyond Cubitt Town, so that section was localised as 277A until 1977. Titans appeared in 1982, but an administrative change in 1984 replaced Clapton's Ts with Ms. Poplar closed in 1985 and Clapton in 1987, obliging reallocation to Ash Grove with Ts again. In 1989 new route D7 replaced the 277 south of Limehouse other than on Sundays, and in 1990 Bow took over, accompanying a rerouteing to Highbury & Islington. New ground was broken, however, with the extension in 1991 from Limehouse to Canary Wharf. West Ham briefly had a share between late 1991 and mid-1992. The Sunday Poplar leg came off in 1993, but in 1994 the 277 was projected from Canary Wharf to Leamouth; this section lasted until 2016 when it was rerouted to Crossharbour. Tridents took over in 1999 and Scanias in 2015, with new E40H MMCs in 2017. In 2018 the route was withdrawn west of Dalston Junction. Garage swaps have been common, the 177 moving from Bow to West Ham (2009), back (2011) and to West Ham again (2020).

RIGHT: Seen opposite the second Island Gardens DLR station on 25 June 2020 is Bow's 12407 (YY66 PHN); it would be transferred to West Ham with the 277 two days later.

BELOW: Now with West Ham codes when seen at Mile End on 15 September 2020 is 12408 (YY66 PHO).

278

Heathrow Airport Central, Hayes & Harlington Station, Church Road, Hayes End, Long Lane, Hillingdon Station, Ickenham, West Ruislip, Ruislip (High Street).

ABELLIO (WS) – Alexander Dennis E40H and Enviro400

New at the end of 2019, route 278 replaced the 140 between Heathrow Airport and Hayes & Harlington Station and then continued on to Ruislip via Hayes End and Hillingdon, reprising the 98A of old. Abellio are in charge with a mix of mid-career Enviro400s and new hybrid E40Hs.

LEFT: Returned off lease but then re-acquired by Abellio before a competitor could get hold of it, E40H 2413 (SN61 DGV) is coming up to Hayes & Harlington station on 18 July 2021.

BELOW: One of the new bus complement for the 278, Hayes garage's 2009 (SN69 ZRR) is setting off from Heathrow Central bus station on the afternoon of 29 May 2021.

279

Manor House Station, Seven Sisters, Tottenham, Edmonton, Ponders End, Enfield Highway, Waltham Cross (Bus Station).

ARRIVA LONDON NORTH (E) – Alexander Dennis E40D (T)

Busy trolleybus route 679 gave way in 1960 to new Edmonton RM-operated 279 linking Smithfield and Waltham Cross, with Saturday runs onward to Flamstead End. In 1963 these journeys were extended to Hammond Street, but 1966 saw the off-peak service cut back to Ponders End. A significant boost in 1970 saw the Monday to Friday service extended to Hammond Street and an allocation introduced from Enfield, plus a Sunday Holloway share that lasted six months. To service Sunday market traffic, the 279 on that day of the week was diverted to West Smithfield in 1971 and then, in 1972, to Liverpool Street, but this became part of new OMO DMS route 279A in 1973, the main route falling back to Holloway on Sundays. In 1976 the Sunday service was extended to Hammond Street as well, but this extra-London section was localised as 283 between 1978 and 1980. In the interim the 279 had been withdrawn outright on Sundays, the 279A gaining RMs as a through route. The service north of Waltham Cross was taken off for good in 1985 and Edmonton closed in 1986, leaving just Enfield garage to convert the 279 to OPO in 1986 with Ms. 1992 saw a severe hack that took the 279 off altogether south of Holloway, leaving just an early morning rump to Smithfield until 1996. DLPs and DLAs replaced the Ms in 1999 and witnessed the 279's further curtailment at Manor House in 2004. Ts (E40Ds) took over in 2012 and remain in charge.

RIGHT: Edmonton Green has undergone substantial changes; on 11 March 2020 Enfield's T 241 (LJ61 LKM) negotiates the revised roundabout.

BELOW: One stop further to the south at Edmonton Police Station, T 227 (LJ61 CFX) displays the newest Arriva logo on 24 November 2019.

280

Belmont Station, Sutton, St. Helier, Mitcham, Tooting Broadway, Tooting (St. George's Hospital).

LONDON GENERAL (AL) – Volvo B5LH (WHV)

With the 80's diversion to Morden in 1969, new Sutton RT-operated 280 was commenced to continue the link to Mitcham and Tooting. In 1974 it was converted to OMO with DMSs, and in 1976 its forays south of Belmont to Walton-on-the-Hill were replaced by a full-time extension to Lower Kingswood. However, the inability or reluctance of Surrey County Council to subsidise LT routes going into their territory obliged the 280 to fall back to Belmont in 1982, with Sunday trips to Banstead Hospital that lasted until 1988. Instead, expansion to the north ensued when, in 1985, the 220's section coming from Wandsworth was taken over. In 1988 the route was withdrawn between Sutton Station and Belmont and reallocated from Sutton to Merton garage, exempting it from the travails of Suttonbus. Ms replaced the DMSs in 1991, the same year that saw the 280 altered at both ends, regaining the Belmont leg but being withdrawn between Tooting and Wandsworth in favour of a diversion to Colliers Wood. This terminus was quickly firmed up as St George's Hospital. The Ms gave way to PVLs in 2000 and two contracts later a mix of mid-life Es and WVLs filtered into action. For the 2017 contract with London General, WHV-class Volvo B5LH hybrids were cascaded south after the loss of the 19.

LEFT: Merton's Volvo B5LH WHV 22 (LJ61 NVH), missing its Go-Ahead logo on the front, is crossing Tooting Broadway on 30 July 2020.

BELOW: WHV 22 (LJ61 NVH) still hasn't had any frontal logos applied when captured on the new road layout in Mitcham on 9 May 2021.

281

Hounslow (Bus Station), Whitton, Twickenham, Fulwell, Teddington, Hampton Wick, Kingston, Surbiton, Ewell Road, Tolworth (Ewell Road).

LONDON UNITED (FW) – Scania N230UD (SP)

The direct replacement for trolleybus route 601 in 1962, the 281 has been a strong fixture ever since. It has always been operated by Fulwell, at first with RMs; in 1965 it was extended from Twickenham to Hounslow over part of the 73 and in 1970 received an extension to Chessington Industrial Estate south of Tolworth. OMO on Sundays was introduced in 1972 with SMs (later DMSs and Ms) but the rest didn't follow until 1982, when Ms took over daily. The Chessington Industrial Estate leg came off in 1987 and a Hounslow share appeared between 1991 and 1996. The Ms gave way to Volvo Olympians (VAs) in 1998, with Tridents (TAs) following in 2003, Scanias (SPs) in 2014 and, with London United's latest contract, new electric BYDs (BCEs) are expected.

RIGHT: On the afternoon of 7 March 2021, Fulwell's SP 40109 (YR59 FYO) is coming through Kingston, but will unfortunately be avoiding Eden Street in the interests of social distancing.

282

Ealing Hospital, Greenford, Yeading, Northolt, Field End Road, Eastcote, Northwood Hills, Northwood, Mount Vernon Hospital.

METROLINE WEST (G) – Alexander Dennis E40H (TEH)

New in 1968 to take over the 232's far end, Southall's 282 fielded MBs, then DMSs (1974) and Ms (1979). Hanwell took over in 1986 and minibuses (RWs) came in 1990. Greenford have run the route since 1993, converting it to DM in 1998, to TN in 2003 (these becoming Metroline TPs in 2013), then to TEs and, since 2020, hybrid TEHs.

RIGHT: Refurbished for the 282, Greenford's E40H TEH 1459 (LK13 BHE) passes through Greenford on 30 March 2021.

283

East Acton (Brunel Road), Bloemfontein Road, Uxbridge Road, Shepherd's Bush, Hammersmith (Bus Station).

LONDON UNITED (S) – Alexander Dennis E20D (DLE)

In 1983 a need was identified for a bus service through the White City Estate, so the 283 was introduced with four Shepherd's Bush DMSs and an eastern terminus at Fulham Broadway. Ms took over later in the year and in 1984 the route was diverted to West Brompton. Between 1986 and 1989 Scancoaches operated the 283 with unusual Jonckheere-bodied Scanias, but after that LBL returned as contractor with new Leyland Lynxes put into Shepherd's Bush. In 1990 the LXs passed with the route to Stamford Brook garage, leaving when the route was converted to DT operation in 1991 and withdrawn between Hammersmith and West Brompton. A useful extension south took the route to Barnes Pond in 1992, though this lasted only a year the first time. Shepherd's Bush garage took back the 283 in 1996 and was in charge when the Barnes extension returned in 1998; two years after that, it was modified so that it terminated at the Wetland Centre during that attraction's opening hours. Stamford Brook resumed control in 1998 and converted the 283 to new Dart SLFs (DPSs) when contract renewal with the incumbent London United was secured in 2002. In 2009 NCP Challenger won the 283 and introduced new Optare Versas, but this company (known latterly as NSL) was taken over by London United and the buses absorbed, together with their garage at Park Royal. In 2016 the Barnes leg was transferred to the 485 and in 2017 the new Park Royal site commenced operations. New E20Ds appeared over the cusp of 2018/19.

LEFT: On 23 May 2019 DLE 30049 (SN17 MUP), recently transferred from Shepherd's Bush to the new Park Royal, is coming up to Hammersmith.

BELOW: Within Hammersmith Low Level bus station, distinct from the High Level premises, is DLE 30326 (YX68 UVM) on 5 January 2019.

284

Lewisham (Town Centre), Ladywell, Ravensbourne Park, Catford, Sangley Road, Verdant Lane, Downham, Grove Park, Grove Park Cemetery.

STAGECOACH SELKENT (KB) – Alexander Dennis E20D

New in 1989, the 284 tapped unserved ground west of Lewisham and Catford before picking up the 124's path to Grove Park. It began with MW-class Mercedes-Benz 811Ds from Catford garage, with SRs helping. In 1994 it was tendered and awarded to Kentish Bus with Optare Metroriders, but the new operator had overreached itself and struggled; moving bases from Lewisham and back didn't help, and late in 1995 the 284 was surrendered and Metrobus stepped in, taking on the Metroriders themselves. Since then it's been a straight fight for control between Metrobus and Stagecoach Selkent; the latter won in 2001 and introduced new Dart SLFs (SLDs), but Metrobus returned in 2006 with Optare Esteem-bodied Scanias. The contract was defended successfully and in 2013 was provisioned with new E20Ds, but in 2018 Stagecoach Selkent won again. E20Ds of MMC style are the staple, but a new garage at Kangley Bridge Road in Lower Sydenham was opened to operate them.

RIGHT: With the second Lewisham bus station now obliterated by a pair of office blocks, westbound routes now have to wend their way round their perimeter towards a new stand behind the railway tracks. That's where 36681 (YY67 UUB) is going on 14 December 2018.

BELOW: Coming through Catford on 23 August 2020 is Kangley Bridge Road's 36683 (YY67 UUD).

285

Heathrow Airport Central, Hatton Cross, Feltham, Hanworth, Hampton Hill, Teddington, Hampton Wick, Kingston (Cromwell Road Bus Station).

ABELLIO (TF) – Alexander Dennis E40D

New in 1962, the 285 replaced trolleybus route 605 with a projection on beyond Teddington to London Airport (as was) and an eastern remit as far as Haydons Road. Fulwell operated RMs, though Merton had an intermittent Sunday allocation with RTs, and in 1966 Norbiton joined in. The eastern leg was pulled back at this time to New Malden, with infrequent runs on to New Malden or Wimbledon, and SMS OMO in 1971 saw the 285's curtailment at Kingston, with New Malden served only in the peaks. This endured for a decade, though Norbiton was reduced to Sundays only. DMSs restored the upper deck from both garages in 1975 and the New Malden leg was restored to all-day. Ms took over in 1979 and Norbiton withdrew in 1982, but in 1987 the New Malden leg was taken off outside the peaks again, finally disappearing in 1990 when the rest of the route was converted to Darts (DTs and then a DT/DR mix). In 1996 London Buslines won the contract and put new yellow Darts on; five years later London United came back, but Hounslow Heath was now the operating garage and introduced new DPS-class Dart SLFs. These were replaced by DEs (Enviro200s) in 2008 and by Volvo B5LH double-deckers in 2015. In 2020 Abellio took over, hiring Stagecoach E40Ds until its own new examples came.

LEFT: The 285's new buses were held up by the pandemic-related shutdown of factory production, but when the frst lockdown was lifted came to Twickenham and replaced hired Stagecoach E40Ds. On 8 August 2020 new 2040 (SK20 BEU) is in the westbound bus contraflow at Kingston.

BELOW: 2052 (SK20 BFV) nears Kingston on 7 March 2021.

286

Greenwich (Cutty Sark), East Greenwich, Westcombe Park, Blackheath, Kidbrooke, Eltham, Avery Hill, Sidcup, Queen Mary's Hospital.

LONDON CENTRAL (MG) – Wrightbus Streetlite (WS)

Replacing the 108's unsuccessful Eltham section in 1986, the 286 began with New Cross Ts before being reallocated later in the year to Sidcup and then back to New Cross when Sidcup closed. Minibuses came in 1989 in the form of transferred SRs, and in 1992 when Transcity took over the contract, along came green Dennis Darts. These were repainted cream and maroon upon Kentish Bus's acquisition of Transcity the following year, and in 1998 new Dart SLFs in the livery of Arriva Kent Thameside came to replace them. At this point the 286 was extended from Eltham to Queen Mary's Hospital via Sidcup and still serves that facility. For its contract renewal in 2007, new Enviro200s in red were delivered, and when the route was won by London Central in 2014, new E20Ds were the staple, working out of New Cross. However, in 2017, these were diverted to the 170, whose new Streetlites were deemed too high for a low bridge in Battersea, and the WSs have been in charge since then. At the same time, the 286 found itself reallocated from New Cross to Morden Wharf.

RIGHT: On 17 April 2021 in Eltham High Street we see Morden Wharf's WS 106 (SK67 FMD).

BELOW: Just passing Eltham station on 17 April 2021, WS 104 (SK67 FMA) was new to Stockwell but spent less than five weeks on the 170 before transferring to the 286 at New Cross, and thence to Morden Wharf.

287

Rainham (Abbey Wood Lane), Rainham, Dagenham, Ripple Road, Barking Station.

STAGECOACH EAST LONDON (RM) – Alexander Dennis E40D

New in 1982 to take over the southern bore of the 87, the 287 would end up outliving its parent. On introduction it was operated by Barking-based Titans, though the western terminus fluctuated from Becontree to Becontree Heath and even Marks Gate (1987) before falling back in 1991, whereupon it was rerouted to Ilford. The Barking-Ilford leg proved shortlived, coming off when tendering deposited the 287 with Docklands Transit in 1993; Mercedes-Benz 811D minibuses were used. Stagecoach bought Docklands Transit in 1997 and brought Darts (PDs) from Oxford to take over the 287 out of Barking. Between 1998 and 2001 the route was projected from Barking station to serve Harts Lane Estate, but this stopped when the 368 took over that section. In the same year new Dart SLFs (SLDs) took over, and after a decade came new Enviro400s to convert the route back to double-deck in accordance with a retained Stagecoach East London contract. Rainham garage now took over, and this combination has endured across another contract award, made in 2018.

LEFT: On a sunny 17 July 2019 Rainham's 19837 (LX61 DDJ) stages through Barking.

BELOW: Coming back in the other direction on 17 July 2021 is 19832 (LX11 BMU), which has just negotiated the fiddly hairpin constructed so that Barking's marketplace could be pedestrianised.

288

Queensbury (Morrisons), Queensbury Station, Camrose Avenue, Edgware, Broadfields Estate.

SOVEREIGN (BT) – Alexander Dennis E20D (DLE)

Introduced in 1972 with one Edgware SMS, the 288 ran up to the Broadfields Estate, looped round it and came back to Edgware Station. And so it continued for the next two decades, though in 1980 Ms replaced the Swifts and in 1990 DTs supplanted the Metrobuses. It was only in 1993 that the 288 broke out of its box through an extension to Queensbury over the old 107's furthest extent. DRs were the favoured type of Dart across the privatisation of Metroline, and in 1996 these gave way to EDRs. In 2001 low-floor Dart SLFs (DLD class) took over, but in 2006 Arriva the Shires won the contract, giving rise to the lunacy of operating from Garston, eight miles away, when the former garage was right on line of route. New DAF SB120s were the staple and remained so for two contracts, after which Garston closed in 2018 and Sovereign took over, based inside the two-company Edgware garage. New E20Ds of DLE class are now in charge.

RIGHT: On 2 September 2018, a day after entering service, Sovereign's DLE 30264 (SK68 LUA) is swinging into Edgware bus station, now halfway along the 288.

BELOW: DLE 30253 (SN18 KWC) is coming up to Edgware on 20 July 2020.

289

Purley Station, Purley Way, Thornton Road, Thornton Heath Pond, West Croydon, Lower Addiscombe Road, Woodside, Elmers End Station.

ARRIVA LONDON SOUTH (TH) – Alexander Dennis E20D (ENX)

New in 1968, the 289 inherited a short section of the 50 that operated across the top of Croydon to Addiscombe; four RTs from Thornton Heath were in charge. SMSs converted it to OMO in 1970 and in 1973 it was rerouted to serve Croydon itself. In 1974 an extension took the 289 to Elmers End and four years later it was pushed on to Beckenham Junction, doubling the PVR at a stroke. This was when Elmers End garage replaced Thornton Heath as operator, and shortly after came new LSs. In 1981 the 289 grew again with another extension, this time from the Thornton Heath end over the 115 to Purley. However, in 1985 the Elmers End-Beckenham Junction leg was withdrawn; a year later Elmers End garage closed and up stepped Croydon. Tendering in 1987 turned the 289 over to London Country South West with similar Nationals from Chelsham garage, though what had by 1991 become London & Country restocked it with a mix of Dennis Falcons and Leyland Lynxes and put it into its own Croydon garage. This operation was part of Londonlinks from 1995, and new Dennis Lances took over. These were repainted red when Arriva consolidated operations here in 1998, and PDL-class Dart SLFs were delivered in 2000. Since 2007 Thornton Heath has been back in charge, and for the 2012 renewal phased in new E20Ds.

LEFT: Coming out of Purley station on 11 February 2016 is ENX 19 (LJ12 BYF), allocated to Thornton Heath.

BELOW: With white-character blinds by comparison with the photograph above, ENL 49 (LJ10 CSF) was a later transfer unto Thornton Heath and on 25 April 2017 is seen at West Croydon.

290

Staines (Bus Station), Ashford, School Road, Ashford Common, Sunbury Cross, Hanworth, Fulwell, Twickenham Station.

ABELLIO (TF) – Alexander Dennis E20D

The modern 290 has shifted geographically away from its origins in 1970 as a Hammersmith-Richmond service with four RFs from Twickenham. Its first change was reallocation to Riverside upon Twickenham's closure that same year, and in 1976 BLs replaced the RFs. In 1982 the 290 gained the basis of its current form with an extension over the 90 to Richmond, reallocation to Fulwell and conversion to Ms, and this status quo continued throughout the decade, but in 1990 the Richmond-Hammersmith section was turned over to new route 190, rendering the rump of the 290 susceptible for demotion to Darts (DR) in 1992. Only on Sundays did the 290 continue to reach Hammersmith, with peak journeys as far as Chiswick, but in 1997 the route's eastern terminus was standardised as Richmond. The link with its beginnings was completely broken when the 290 was withdrawn between Twickenham and Richmond in 2001, and the following year DPS-class Dart SLFs introduced low-floor operation. In 2011 the route was tendered and awarded to Abellio, which put into service new E20Ds from Twickenham (physically, the western half of the divided Fulwell garage), and this situation endures today.

RIGHT: 8582 (YX61 GBE) is in Twickenham when seen on the afternoon of 1 August 2021.

BELOW: On 1 August 2021 Twickenham garage's 8579 (YX61 GAU) is coming up to Staines bus station at the far western end of the 290.

291

Woolwich Common (Queen Elizabeth Hospital), Repository Road, Woolwich, Raglan Road, Plumstead Common, Woodlands Estate.

LONDON CENTRAL (MG) – Alexander Dennis E40D (E)

Created in 1981 by taking the old 192 from Woodlands Estate and fusing it with the 151, the 291 thus probed through to Lewisham. Plumstead garage commenced it with MDs and a year later introduced Titans, but in 1984 the route lost its Woolwich-Lewisham section to the 178 and settled as a shuttle. Ls gradually replaced Ts over 1986, when it was twinned with the 244 and buses thus changed their blinds at Woolwich, but in 1988 minibuses beckoned when the 291 became part of the Bexleybus network. These were blue and cream Iveco Dailys (RHs) and MCW Metroriders (OVs). Bexleyheath kept hold of the 291 upon retender in 1991, but as a London Central operation rather than a Selkent one. In 1993 new Optare Metroriders (MRLs) were delivered and saw out five more years before tendering restored Plumstead as a Stagecoach Selkent operation, with new Dart SLFs (SLDs). A second batch of these was in charge from 2003 and Enviro200s after that, but in 2018 London Central was awarded the contract and the opportunity was taken to double-deck the 291, with Es from the new Morden Wharf premises. This was intended to tie in with the opening of the Elizabeth line, which has still to happen.

LEFT: New to New Cross and spending its first five years on the 36, E 264 (SN62 DFL) was replaced in 2018 and refurbished for a quieter life on the 178 and 291. It is seen at Woolwich on 31 October 2020.

BELOW: Coming round the much-improved road layout at Woolwich on 28 February 2021 is Modern Wharf's E 268 (SN62 DHA).

292

Borehamwood (Rossington Avenue), Theobald Street, Borehamwood, Barnet Way, Apex Corner, Edgware, Burnt Oak, Colindale (Asda).

METROLINE (HD) – Volvo B9TL (VW)

Introduced in 1962 to take the top end off the 52, the 292, with its Edgware-based RTs, got as far south as Willesden before being pulled back to Colindale in 1965. OMO DMSs took over in 1973, with most of the service curtailed at Edgware but a bifurcation added to Grahame Park. Ms replaced the DMSs in 1980 and continued until the advent of tendering, which saw the 292 lost to London Country North East in 1987. This operation, with LRs from St Albans, proved so fraught, however, that the route was reassigned to BTS in 1988 and the newcomer proved to be a success story, replacing its stopgap Nationals with Atlanteans and then new Scanias. LBL gained back the 292 when it was offered out again, restoring Edgware M operation, but in 1998 Sovereign, heirs to BTS here, were put in charge again and this time with new blue Volvo Olympians. These were replaced by existing VAs when London United bought Sovereign in 2002 and, shortly after, new VLP-class Volvo B7TLs brought the 292 into the low-floor era. Scanias of SLE class replaced those in turn. In 2018 a third tour of duty from Edgware came into being when Metroline won the route once more, this time gathering mid-career Volvo B9TLs (VWs). Later in 2021 the 292 was reallocated from Edgware to Harrow Weald garage.

RIGHT: Just transferred from Edgware to Harrow Weald and turning onto the main road on 5 September 2021, VW 1208 (LK61 BMZ) has a wing still in factory black.

BELOW: It's the opposite wing that's still black on fellow Harrow Weald Volvo B9TL VW 1201 (LK11 CYV), seen on 5 September 2021 in Edgware.

293

Morden Station, Hillcross Avenue, Lower Morden, Garth Road, North Cheam, Ewell, Epsom, Epsom General Hospital.

LONDON UNITED (TV) – Alexander Dennis E20D (DXE)

A Morden-Epsom link from its establishment in 1970, the 293 has grown and shrunk in either direction. At its start it was MB-operated from Merton garage and continued northward to Wimbledon in the peaks. 1974 saw DMSs give it an upper deck and in 1982 it was reallocated to Sutton garage, and in 1983 its frst major change saw it rerouted at Morden to Hackbridge. Merton took it back in 1985, but in 1986 it was put out to tender and scooped up by London Country, with Atlanteans from Dorking. In 1989 the 293's Morden-Hackbridge section was separated out as 393 and the northern terminus became Merton Abbey. Leatherhead garage took over operation from 1990, increasingly with newer Volvo Citybuses and including garage runs from Epsom. By now it had fallen out of the LRT system altogether, but in 2000 was gathered back in, coming under London General's stewardship with Sutton Ms. In 2003 it was retendered and passed to Epsom Buses (Quality Line), who introduced new Mercedes-Benz Citaros and implemented an intermediate rerouting from Morden via Garth Road. Metrobus operated the route with Scanias between 2008 and 2018 after which Quality Line came back, now as an RATP subsidiary, with the longest E20Ds. In 2021 it transferred to Tolworth at London United.

LEFT: RATP have been removing buses' company identities in favour of a straightforward RATP Group fleetname, but an interim step is just peeling off the surplus, which Quality Line was by the time Tolworth's DXE 30287 (SK68 LXU) was seen at Epsom on 28 June 2021.

BELOW: On 16 July 2021 DXE 30284 (SK68 LXR) is two stops further back in Epsom.

294

Havering Park (Firbank Road), Lodge Lane, Collier Row, Romford, Gidea Park Station, Harold Wood, Gooshays Drive, Harold Hill, Whitchurch Road, Noak Hill (Tees Drive).

STAGECOACH EAST LONDON (NS) – Alexander Dennis E40D

New in 1970 to replace part of the 66, the 294 quickly exchanged its North Street RTs for OMO SMSs; the upper deck returned in 1976 with DMSs and in 1979 Titans took over. In 1986 it was diverted from Hornchurch to Gidea Park over the 247, but in 1988 was pulled back from there to Noak Hill. After two decades of Ts, Tridents took over in 2000 and those achieved almost the same lifespan, coming off in 2016 in favour of today's E40D MMCs.

RIGHT: Remarkably stable in the modern era, the 294 has only ever worked out of North Street, company changes notwithstanding. On 2 February 2020 its 10341 (SN16 OLB) is seen at Harold Wood station.

BELOW: On a sun-drenched 13 September 2020 10340 (SN16 OKZ) is at Romford station.

295

Ladbroke Grove (Sainsbury's), Shepherd's Bush, Hammersmith, Fulham Broadway, Wandsworth Bridge, York Road, Plough Road, Clapham Junction (Falcon Road).

METROLINE WEST (WJ) – Volvo B5LH (VWH)

Introduced in 1967 as an East Acton-Hammersmith local, the 295 came into its own with an extension south to Wandsworth in 1968. Shepherd's Bush's five RMs were replaced in 1972 by six OMO DMSs and operation reallocated to Wandsworth garage. Later that year the route was diverted at the north to the familiar Ladbroke Grove direction and grew steadily with the extension south from Wandsworth to Clapham Junction in 1975; three years later its Saturday service was projected on further still, to Battersea Park, and in 1979 this was rendered daily, though it was pulled back again in 1981. Ms replaced DMSs in 1983 and Wandsworth's closure in 1987 compelled reallocation to Westbourne Park, though it had moved again to Shepherd's Bush by year's end. In 1992 the 295 was single-decked with Darts (DRLs) and reallocated to Victoria Basement; Battersea Bridge inherited these in 1994 but closed in 1998, at which point Ms returned from Stockwell to restore the upper deck. In 2000 First's contract win was implemented with new Dennis Dart SLFs (DMLs) out of Westbourne Park, but double-deckers returned again in 2003 as TNs. Tower Transit bought First's operations here in 2013 and continued until 2015, when Metroline West won and introduced new VWHs from Willesden Junction.

LEFT: Willesden Junction's Wrightbus Gemini 3-bodied Volvo B5LH VWH 2133 (LK65 EBO) leaves Clapham Junction on 8 December 2020.

BELOW: Two of the 295's usual complement, seen at Clapham Junction on 8 December 2020, are VWHs 2133 (LK65 EBO) and 2136 (LK65 EBV).

296

Ilford Broadway (Sainsbury's), Gants Hill, Newbury Park, Little Heath, Rose Lane, Romford Station.

STAGECOACH EAST LONDON (NS) – Alexander Dennis Enviro200

New in 1982 to replace the 66 east of Romford, the 296 began with Titans from North Street garage and in 1987 was extended over the 66A and 139 to Ilford. 1992 saw it won by Capital Citybus with new yellow Leyland Olympians from Dagenham, which remained in charge through a company change to First Capital and livery change to red in 1998. In 2000 it was withdrawn east of Romford, rendering it quiet enough for single-decking, which took place in 2001 with Dart SLFs. Stagecoach won control in 2005 and North Street returned with its own Dart SLFs; this garage has stayed put ever since, with E20Ds forming the modern runout.

RIGHT: On 17 July 2021 North Street's 36261 (LX11 AVR), carrying Stagecoach's latest corporate logos, is seen at Romford station.

297

Willesden Garage, Neasden Lane, Neasden, Wembley Park, Wembley Central, Alperton, Perivale, Argyle Road, Castlebar Road, Ealing Broadway Station.

METROLINE (PA) – Volvo B9TL (VW)

New in 1968 as a Perivale local, the 297 began with Alperton RTs; MB OMO came in 1969, DMSs in 1972 and Ms in 1980. In 1982 Willesden took over and in 1984 the route was extended to Ealing Broadway. Darts (DWs) came in 1990, back at Alperton, followed in 1995 by DPs. Under Metroline from 1998, it used Willesden DLDs and was then double-decked in 2003 with TPs from Perivale. In 2009 Perivale West took over with TEs and then introduced SEL-class Scanias; today's offering comprises VW-class Volvo B9TLs.

RIGHT: On 11 April 2021 Perivale West's VW 1188 (LK11 CXY) is at Ealing, Argyle Road.

298

Arnos Grove Station, Waterfall Road, Southgate, Cockfosters, Stagg Hill, Potters Bar, Mutton Lane, Potters Bar Station.

SULLIVAN BUSES (SM) – Alexander Dennis E20D (AE)

New in 1968 to clip the top off the 29 at its greatest extent, the 298 has known great rises and falls since then. Early Potters Bar operation gave way in 1970 to a share between Palmers Green and Wood Green garages with RMs and in 1971 Palmers Green took over sole control. In 1973 the route was withdrawn between Turnpike Lane and Finsbury Park, though this section was restored again between 1975 and 1977. OMO came in 1980 with DMSs and now from Wood Green and Potters Bar; the former upgraded to Ms in 1981 and the latter in 1982. The proportion of work by each garage fluctuated thereafter, but in 1986 the 298 was tendered and London Country won it with LRs from St Albans. This garage came under London Country North East later that year but struggled desperately to the extent that the route was taken off them in 1988. Grey-Green stepped up and were much better; Fleetlines were the staple, followed by Metrobuses. In 1992 the route was split across Southgate and minibussed under Capital Citybus with Optare Metroriders. Cowie Leaside won it in 1997 and restored Palmers Green operation before settling it at Wood Green in 1998; Darts (LDRs) manned it until 2003 when DAF SB120s (DWLs) took over. During this time the 298 was withdrawn from South Mimms but projected from Southgate to Arnos Grove. Since 2012 Sullivan Buses has been in charge, using E20Ds (AEs).

LEFT: Sullivan Buses vehicles all have personalised registrations with SUL as the basis. Leaving Arnos Grove on 21 July 2021 is AE 20 (DS66 SUL), an MMC E20D from the later batch new to the W9.

BELOW: The 298's usual contingent of E20Ds is represented just north of Southgate by AE 13 (KR61 SUL) on 31 July 2021.

299

Muswell Hill Broadway, Durnsford Road, Bounds Green, Powys Lane, Southgate, Avenue Road, Reservoir Road, Cockfosters Station.

SULLIVAN BUSES (SM) – Wrightbus Streetlite (SL)

New in 1992, the 299 was an offshoot of the 298 created to give service to Reservoir Road in outer Southgate and then take on the W9's old home stretch to Muswell Hill. It was operated by Capital Citybus from Northumberland Park with Optare Metroriders, which changed their livery from yellow to red and yellow when Capital Citybus became First Capital in 1998. In 2001 new DM-class Dennis Dart SLFs appeared and with the next contract new Enviro200s of the same length took over. When Northumberland Park was taken over by London General in 2013 these DMSs became SENs, but in 2018 the 299 was won by Sullivan Buses and provisioned with new Wrightbus Streetlites.

RIGHT: Although carrying no fleetnames, Sullivan Buses bring distinctiveness to the scene through their batches of personalised registrations, like that on SL 95 (MH67 SUL), seen at Southgate station on 3 November 2019.

BELOW: On 8 September 2019 SL 91 (JF67 SUL) is north of Muswell Hill. Route 299 feeds the 389 and 399 pair in Barnet.

300

Canning Town (Bus Station), Prince Regent Lane, Stansfeld Road, Beckton, Vicarage Lane, Park Avenue, East Ham (Wordsworth Avenue).

BLUE TRIANGLE (RR) – Alexander Dennis E20D (SE)

New in 1993 as part of a large package of changes in the London Borough of Newham, the 300 brought buses to some unserved streets between East Ham and Cyprus, with Upton Park SRs put in charge. DRLs took over in 1995, shortly after the garage came under Stagecoach East London at privatisation, and in 1999 the allocation was moved to Barking, but later that year the route was revamped, forsaking the Cyprus section in favour of an extension over the 276 to Canning Town. Barking's complement by now was PD-class Darts ex-Thames Transit, and after that came ALX200-bodied Dennis Dart SLFs (first known as SLDs, then DMs, then without class codes at all). Upton Park gained back the 300 in 2009, but closed a year later with the 300's award to Go-Ahead. Since that time E20Ds (SEs) have been in charge, shuffled as needed between Rainham, Silvertown and River Road.

LEFT: Fresh from repaint out of its original livery of red with charcoal grey skirt, SE 95 (SN11 FGA) turns into East Ham High Street on 21 April 2019.

BELOW: On 27 March 2021 River Road-based SE 97 (SN11 FGD) swings out of Beckton bus station.